CORNYATION

CORNYATION

San Antonio's Outrageous Fiesta Tradition

Amy L. Stone

Maverick Books / Trinity University Press

San Antonio

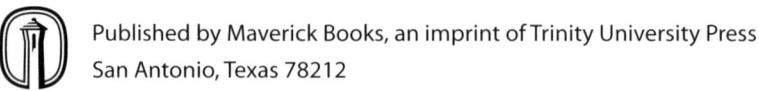

Published by Maverick Books, an imprint of Trinity University Press
San Antonio, Texas 78212

Book design by Anne Richmond Boston

Cover art: Front, Jeanie Muerer as Queen of the Garden Patches, 1955.
Courtesy of the Institute of Texan Cultures.

ISBN 978-1-59534-800-5 paper
ISBN 978-1-59534-801-2 ebook
Printed in China

Trinity University Press strives to produce its books using methods and materials in an environmentally sensitive manner. We favor working with manufacturers that practice sustainable management of all natural resources, produce paper using recycled stock, and manage forests with the best possible practices for people, biodiversity, and sustainability. The press is a member of the Green Press Initiative, a nonprofit program dedicated to supporting publishers in their efforts to reduce their impacts on endangered forests, climate change, and forest-dependent communities.

The paper used in this publication meets the minimum requirements
of the American National Standard for Information Sciences—Permanence of Paper for
Printed Library Materials, ANSI 39.48–1992.

CIP data on file at the Library of Congress
21 20 19 18 17 | 5 4 3 2 1

To Robert Rehm, Mark Steckly, Pat Wells, and Michael Marmontello.

May the afterlife be filled with tasty food, campy drag, and people who exit the stage properly.

Mark, thank you for teaching me that if it's not fun, you're doing it wrong.

CONTENTS

INTRODUCTION

In 2009 a co-worker suggested that I attend a show called "Cornyation" in downtown San Antonio during its annual Fiesta, a ten-day celebration across the city of parties, parades, and festival royalty. Despite rumors that Cornyation had sold out, I managed to buy a ticket at the last minute to the Tuesday night show. Entering the Charline McCombs Empire Theatre in the heart of San Antonio, I was in awe of the size of the venue, with its almost thousand-seat capacity. Excited adult spectators wearing colorful hats and sashes or vests covered in medals from Fiesta San Antonio events packed the theater's three tiers. Some people carried *cascarones*, eggs filled with confetti, which they tossed at each other during intermission. The diversity of the crowd impressed me. Heterosexual couples, Latino gay men, dressed-up senior citizens, black lesbian couples, and, beside me, a charming white straight suburban couple all shared the theater space.

As I settled into my seat to watch the show, the royalty of the event, the "King Anchovy," appeared—San Antonio's city manager, Sheryl Sculley, decked out in a skintight red body suit, floor-length cape, and stiletto boots. This event was obviously going to be something special. Sculley danced around the stage as the master of ceremonies announced that it was time to "let the queens be unleashed!" The city manager-turned-royal then presided over an hour-long show of skits and performances that mocked everything from reality television to national politics to a raid on a Texas Mormon compound to San Antonio tourism. Throughout the night, a cast of more than one hundred took the stage in all manner of costumes. Ballet San Antonio performers danced a satirical version of the "Danse des petits cygnes" from *Swan Lake*, in which the ballet dancers turned into ducks before being mowed down by a San Antonio River Walk touring boat. I laughed so hard that my cheeks hurt.

City Manager Sheryl Sculley as King Anchovy, 2009.

A newspaper article the next day reported: "There is probably nowhere else where the city manager goes by the name King Anchovy, dresses up as Superwoman and shares a stage with drag queens doing raunchy spoofs of everything from an upcoming mayoral election to a raid on a polygamist ranch. Through Thursday, San Antonio—at least some of San Antonio—is proud to be that place."[1] The cast repeated the show five more times over the next two evenings, raising more than $120,000 for local charities, most of which were HIV/AIDS service organizations.[2] Michelle Durham, the director of one of the beneficiaries, BEAT AIDS, a small nonprofit focused on HIV prevention and testing in the black community, proclaimed when she received her $35,000 check that "we can't survive without it." Her organization had almost shut its doors the previous month due to lack of funds.[3]

That night there were so many things that I found interesting about Cornyation: the diversity of people who enjoyed the show, the visibility of gay artistry and drag queens, and the biting humor of the skits. What really struck me, though, was that the show had begun in the 1950s, according to my program. I had so many questions. Had the show always been this irreverent and campy? Had it always been performed for such a diverse audience? I set off to answer these questions, embarking on several years of research into the history of the show. I discovered that long before performers danced on the Empire Theatre stage,

Jeanie Muerer as Queen of the Garden Patches, designed by Leslie Wilk, 1955.

Cornyation was performed in the 1950s and 1960s for family audiences numbering in the thousands at the Fiesta event A Night in Old San Antonio. In the early 1960s the show was kicked out of its venue; almost two decades passed before it was revived in the 1980s. In 2015 the Cornyation cast put on the fiftieth performance of the show.

WHY CORNY THINGS ARE IMPORTANT

This book is the first substantive history of Cornyation and one of the only books written about the incorporation of gay men and lesbians into civic festivals like Fiesta. Studying this show helps us understand the complexity of contemporary urban festivals and gay and lesbian incorporation into city life. Most research on LGBT life in U.S. cities focuses on gay bars, neighborhoods, activism, or events like Pride. I argue that Cornyation has contributed to the city of San Antonio and a major civic festival for five decades through fundraising, attracting a diverse audience, and critiquing the status quo with campy satire that renders gay life

Cast photograph, 1963.

visible to the public. I place the show in its broader social context as it operates within the city, the Fiesta event, and the LGBT community.

The show has contributed to the city through fundraising for health- and theater-related charities. In the 1950s and 1960s Cornyation raised funds for the San Antonio Little Theater (SALT), funds that helped the theater company move into and remodel the iconic San Pedro Playhouse theater.[4] In the 1990s the show organizers created their own nonprofit foundation; since then, Cornyation has raised almost two million dollars, funds which have mostly gone to support nonprofit HIV/AIDS service organizations.[5] These donations have been critical for supporting nonprofit organizations that are often underfunded.

Festivals, like Fiesta San Antonio or New Orleans's Mardi Gras, can be a time both of wild festive abandon and of hierarchy and exclusion.[6] Festivals have a history of being a period in which normal rules and obligations are momentarily suspended; these events temporarily create a "world upside-down."[7] For example, during medieval carnivals peasant participants could criticize the

Empress Mary Byall and Aubrey Kline as King Anchovy, 1963.

king, crown their own king, be sacrilegious, and engage in eccentric behavior without concern of retribution.[8] Similarly, during contemporary festivals people engage in behaviors they wouldn't typically, such as eating food from street vendors, drinking more alcohol, having sex with strangers, and buying and wearing gaudy festival apparel. This release has always been an important part of what makes festivals fun. But festivals are not only about release and fun; these events also reinforce and at times challenge the existing power dynamics in a city. There are some important differences between the medieval carnivals described by some scholars and more contemporary festivals like Fiesta San Antonio. Festivals like Fiesta and Mardi Gras are often organized by the city's "heritage elite"—members of the social class considered by the public to be responsible for high culture in the city.

Frequently, the most exclusive events at these celebrations are elitist and tightly controlled. The festival royalty, crowned by organizations to reign over the festivities, come from the richest families in town. King Rex of New Orleans's Mardi Gras and King Antonio of Fiesta are never just ordinary residents of those cities; they are always famous individuals or from a wealthy family. In the case of Fiesta San Antonio, upper-class Anglo women organized the parade that inaugurated the event in 1891 (the parade, known as the Battle of the Flowers, honored the heroes of San Jacinto, the concluding battle in the 1836 Texas Revolution; the parade continues to wind through San Antonio today).[9] Until the 1950s almost all Fiesta events were organized by exclusive societies—such as the Order of the Alamo and the Texas Cavaliers—that were dominated by the heritage elite.[10] One of the most prominent events historically has been the Coronation of the Queen of the Order of the Alamo, a debutante pageant that crowns a queen of the festival.

Marginalized groups, however, can also claim a place for themselves in cities nationwide by asserting their value and importance during citywide festivals.[11] In *Inventing the Fiesta City*, Laura Hernández-Ehrisman traces the changes in Fiesta from its origins to its current state as a ten-day festival with more than one hundred fundraising events throughout the city sponsored by participating organizations. This transformation of Fiesta was partly a consequence of San Antonio residents pressing to make the festival more inclusive by establishing

Cast photograph, 2013.

alternative royalty and creating their own events. Hispanic and black community members pushed for their own royalty figures and for recognition of these figures by the Fiesta San Antonio Commission, which organizes the event. Members of the San Antonio Little Theater created Cornyation as a satire of the Coronation of the Queen of the Order of the Alamo, mocking the elite by crowning their own "duchesses," "empresses," and "queens" in the show.

Through participation in city festivals nationwide, groups marginalized on the bases of gender, race, class, and sexuality can show the rest of their communities their distinct cultural contributions.[12] These cultural contributions—whether they be instructive satire, special foods, costuming, or rituals—allow marginalized groups simultaneously to garner respect for their cultural differences and to claim their right to their cities. Because Fiesta is supposed to bring the city of San Antonio together, I think that who gets included in Fiesta is very important.

In Fiesta San Antonio, Cornyation played a critical role in making the event more inclusive. Whether intentional or not, the show has been part of making gay culture in the city more visible since the 1950s; long before drag queens regularly performed in the show, it included campy gay humor.[13] This increase in visibility parallels the growth of the LGBT community in San Antonio, including the development of lesbian and gay bars in the 1950s and 1960s and the increasing involvement of the LGBT community in Fiesta. The show simultaneously mocks elitism and suggests that gay men are sophisticated critics of the status quo.

Aubrey Davenport as Duchess of the Turkey Trot, designed by John Sharp. Court of the Greater Society, 1965.

Cornyation allowed women and men from across the city to participate in Fiesta, and created a space for campy humor to be performed for a mainstream audience. In addition to the show's significant charity work, three features have made Cornyation especially important: its popularity with a general audience, its criticism of the status quo through satire, and its use of campy gay humor.

Unknown duchess from the 1950s.

A PUBLIC AUDIENCE

In 2010 I went to buy Cornyation tickets the day they went on sale. I woke up at 4:30 AM in order to drive downtown and wait in the long line of eager customers. The line snaked around the corner from the theater box office, which wouldn't open until 10 AM. The mood was cordial; even at this early hour, people greeted one another and watched each other's chairs while they got coffee or breakfast. At the front of the line a group of around ten men and women had reclining camping chairs labeled with their names, several coolers, and a weary look about them. Close to the front was an acquaintance—Brad, a Latino gay man—who

Cornyation camper medal.

had arrived the night before to take his place in line. He explained that the people I'd seen at the front of the line were the "Cornyation campers," a group of hardcore fans eager to be the first to buy tickets for the coveted Thursday late show. They had been showing up earlier than everyone else for years and had made their own medals celebrating their achievement. I waited much farther back, and people passing by on their way to work asked eagerly what show we were waiting for, afraid that they were missing out on tickets. The man next to me replied, "Justin Bieber on Ice"; we all laughed. Within the first hour of ticket sales that day, a theater employee told us that the late Thursday night show had already sold out.

Thousands of people attend Cornyation every year, and this has been the case for five decades. Cornyation has never been a secret spectacle; the show has consistently been covered in local newspapers, reviewed in the society column, and attended by anyone who wanted to buy a ticket. When I conducted interviews for this book, a consistent refrain was that you never knew who might show up to a Cornyation show. It could be your boss, the mayor, or your grandmother. In the 1950s and 1960s everyone from tiny babies on their parents' laps to college students and military men enjoyed the show. After 1982 the audience was primarily adults, as for almost a decade the show was staged in a bar. These adults included people of all different ages, classes, sexualities, races, and genders. Cornyation has always appealed to a diverse audience. In 1997 arts critic Mike Greenberg perhaps summed it up best. "Poised on a thin line between decadence and depravity, Cornyation is the Fiesta event that no decent, respectable citizen would be caught dead at," he wrote. "And a good thing, too. You wouldn't want them spoiling the fun for the rest of us."[14]

A SATIRE OF ELITES AND POLITICS

Cornyation uses humor to critique city politics and elitism. The show began as a satire of social elitism and high culture and has evolved into a parody of popular

Entrance of King Anchovy Christopher Chilton Hill for the fiftieth anniversary show, 2015.

Dana Montana as the Duchess of From My Cold Head Hands and company, designed by Chris Sauter. The Court of the Second Coming, 2013.

culture and politics. According to many contemporary Cornyation performers and designers, no one is safe from their corny satire. Packaged within this comedy and satire is criticism of the status quo, nepotism, extremism, ignorance, elitism, homophobia, and, most of all, bad taste. For more than five decades of performance Cornyation has satirized Fiesta and other city festivals, city officials, social elites, political leaders, celebrities, national politics, and popular culture. It has commemorated major events in San Antonio with attention to changes in the art and theater world. From a 1951 mockery of San Antonio debutante pageantry to a 2013 satire on the National Rifle Association, the show has used humor to critique and parody the status quo.

Scholars are undecided on whether this satire matters; they often dismiss performances, particularly performances during festivals, as insignificant.[15] They

Julia James as the Queen of Nail Polish, designed by Robin Howard, 1953.

argue that because festivals only happen once a year and are thus ephemeral, what happens at them does not impact the city during the rest of the year. But the peculiar style of satire in festivals and at Cornyation in particular may serve as a check on elitism and political power—after all, these forms of satire serve as a criticism by "the people" that is viewed by thousands and is covered in city papers. In the case of Cornyation, the show operates as a barometer of political and social progress that pushes the edge of what is culturally acceptable—not through typical festival satire but with a campy version of it.

A SAFE SPACE FOR CAMPY GAY HUMOR

On the 2014 Cornyation stage, the master of ceremonies announced the finale of the evening: a satire of the debate over allowing gay adults and young men to

Tesa Gonzalez as Vice-Empress of "Elita," 1987.

Michelle Squilla as the Empress of We Don't Need No Stinkin' Badges, 2014.
Designer John McBurney. Court of Festive Fetes and Frivolous Faux Pas, 2014.

be members of the Boy Scouts of America. Emcee Rick Frederick noted that Boy Scout integration is an "apoplectic vision buried deep within the fevered dreams of the Tea Party." His fellow emcee, Elaine Wolff, remarked, "In their nightmare scenario, traditionalists imagine our boys serving rustic, leave-no-trace full-on Eagle Scout realness, looking like that boy who helped you cross the street on the way to Paris' ball," referencing the documentary *Paris Is Burning,* about gay ball culture.[16] The duo then announced the "First Annual Gay Boy Scout Jamboree Extravaganza" as men and women dressed up in Boy Scout uniforms with sequined red ties entered the stage dancing to the song "Boogie Woogie Bugle Boy." The tall skit designer, John McBurney, paraded sassily as the Scout leader to great applause. The performers marched with American flags as Michelle Squilla, the Empress of We Don't Need No Stinkin' Badges, danced between them. The audience went wild as the performers switched their American flags for rainbow Pride flags. This sketch took the sex-related panic over having gay men in the Boy Scouts and transformed it into a playful yet critical spectacle. Rather than hiding or denying any fears of Boy Scout queerness, the audience did the opposite, and cheered at the sight of adult men and women in glittery Scout uniforms grinding against rainbow Pride flags to the Pharrell Williams song "Happy."

Cornyation does not just push the envelope through satire; it is also a *campy* farce. Camp is an expression of lively, audacious artistic style associated with gay

Ann Kinser as the Queen of Scintillating Saturn, designed by Curt Slangal, 1993. ▶

male culture, although it can be performed by anyone. It involves the inversion or reversal of normal aesthetics such as beauty and good taste.[17] Camp is not the same thing as wearing drag, although many drag shows use campy humor and style. Sometimes camp pokes fun at serious subjects, and it is known for addressing taboo topics. In shows like Cornyation, performers use camp to parody the status quo with more glitter, sequins, flamboyance, bad humor, double entendre, and vulgarity than is found in typical satire.

From its beginnings in the 1950s to its fiftieth anniversary show in 2015, Cornyation has been very campy. In the 1950s and 1960s the show's campiness may have been obvious only to the most attuned audience members who understood the double entendres. What is particularly remarkable about the campy quality of the show during this time is that it was cutting-edge nationally. The camp aesthetic was just emerging in places like New York and San Francisco, and was rarely performed for a mainstream audience.[18] In the 1980s the use of camp in Cornyation became brazen, although the script still included significant use of more veiled language through wordplay and double entendre. The show remains a unique blend of corny, campy festival satire. In contemporary shows, the pope is portrayed as a man dressed in glittery priest robes that are stripped off to reveal women's lingerie; men in Boy Scout uniforms wear makeup and rainbow flag paraphernalia; and the city recycling plan is celebrated by drag queens sporting dresses made of recycled materials.

STUDYING CORNY THINGS

The research for this book took me all over San Antonio. I spent time in city historical archives, the homes of current and former participants in Cornyation, and the storage closet of the San Pedro Playhouse. I studied the early years of the show from many angles. My research assistants and I dug through photography archives across the city. I read old newspaper accounts of the show, which I found in online historical databases and in scrapbooks kept in archives. I used the names from those newspaper articles to track down and interview more than two dozen former participants from the 1950s and 1960s, mainly female duchesses who appeared in the show. My assistants and I also spoke with other members of the art and theater scene from this time period and some relatives of past participants. One of my most exciting moments during this research was finding an eighteen-millimeter film of the 1963 show in the home of longtime performer Mary Byall. Through my archival research, I discovered that the Playhouse (formerly SALT) had office files from the 1950s and 1960s Cornyation productions tucked away in a closet. My research assistants and I spent several days searching through these boxes and ultimately discovered old scripts and files from the earliest years of the show. These scripts included lists of all the designers and cast members. We used the genealogy resources at the public library in San Antonio to learn more about these individuals who had participated in the show.

The contemporary version of the show was easier to research, and digging into it involved considerably more frivolity. When I started investigating the show in 2012, the director and stage manager, Pat Wells, generously let me work as a stage hand for two years, which led to my becoming a duchess for two additional years for designer Mark Steckly. This firsthand experience in the running of the show allowed me to connect with performers and understand the endeavor from the inside. I conducted more than forty interviews with current and former Cornyation designers, duchesses, scriptwriters, and fans. I also scanned boxes of old scripts, programs, newspaper clippings, and files kept over the years by director Ray Chavez. Some of the interviews I conducted for this book were with individuals who asked to remain anonymous; when I quote those sources, I do not provide the individual's name or any personal details. Other individuals allowed me the use of their name.

■ ■ ■

I divide this book into five chronological chapters. In the first chapter, I document the creation of Cornyation as a part of a larger family-oriented Fiesta event, A Night in Old San Antonio. From 1951 to 1964, Cornyation duchesses paraded down the steps of an outdoor theater in downtown San Antonio. This chapter focuses on how, in its early years, Cornyation explicitly mocked the Coronation of the Queen of the Order of the Alamo, a debutante pageant, and expanded the diversity of Fiesta participants and organizers. During this period, the show reflected the campy aesthetic of the sophisticated gay men who designed the costumes and program.

In the second chapter, I analyze Cornyation in the 1960s, when its use of camp became more brazen and the show was more explicitly critical of local and national politics. During this time, some performers and designers from the show also participated in a Cornyation drag show held on the outskirts of town at a gay and lesbian bar. Cornyation reached an unprecedented height of popularity before it was unceremoniously kicked out of Night in Old San Antonio in the winter of 1965 for being too vulgar and no longer family-friendly. The show was performed at an alternate venue in 1965 and then abandoned by SALT as a result of low turnout.

Former designers attempted to revive the show in 1979 at its old venue with limited success. In the third chapter, I document the revival of Cornyation in 1982 by two former Cornyation designers, Raymond "Ray" Chavez and Robert Cotham "Bob" Jolly. For eight years the show was performed in the ballroom of the Bonham Exchange, a new disco bar in downtown San Antonio with a predominantly gay and lesbian clientele. This revival shared many of the original show's characteristics, including the use of the show to raise money for SALT, but its different locale and time period meant that the show could be far more explicit than previously.

The final two chapters document the transformation of the show since 1990 into a major San Antonio fundraiser. In the 1990s Cornyation moved to a new theater venue downtown and became independent from SALT; the event began focusing mainly on raising funds to fight the growing HIV/AIDS pandemic. The costuming of the show became bigger and bolder; Cornyation developed a devoted fan following and became known for fan hijinks in the audience, including the throwing of tortillas before and during the show. In the past decades, the King Anchovy role became more visible and involved in fundraising as well.

■■■

Director Ray Chavez in front of set designed by Robert Rehm, 1993. ▶

FIESTA FOR THE LITTLE PEOPLE

THE 1950s

THE *1950s*

Children fidgeted and adults downed the last of their longneck beers as they waited for the show to begin. The sweeping Arneson River Theatre, located in the middle of the Night in Old San Antonio festival's midway, pushed against the edge of the San Antonio River. The river separated the audience from the stage, and a steep, arching bridge allowed some of the spectators to tower over the stage. Audience members clutched thin broadsheet programs, which proclaimed this event to be the "Cornyation of the Order of the A-Corn" celebrating the 1951 "Court of the Cracked Salad Bowl."

Joe Salek, the director of the San Antonio Little Theater, came onto the stage and announced himself as the "Lord High Chef." At the start of the show the Lord High Chef proclaimed: "Ladies and gentleman, we are gathered together this evening to witness a Conclave of Royalty. I, the Lord High Chef, have summoned from the far corners of the Earth . . . Regal Sa-Lady Ingredients, and am prepared to mix—with the aid of my assistants—a COMBINATION TOSSED SALAD the like of which has never been seen before and probably never [will be] again! The culmination of this culinary artistry will be the Crowning of the Salad, The Empress, Herself, by King Anchovy I. Whether you realize it or not you are sitting on the rim of a huge wooden bowl that is . . . slightly cracked."[1]

And cracked it was. As women paraded down the steps of the bridge, resplendent in repurposed theater costumes decorated with household goods, the Lord High Chef announced them as the Duchesses of Parsley and Onions, touting them with flowery language about cooking. The audience howled with

Coverage of 1953 Cornyation show that includes picture of the first King Anchovy, Howard Bumbaugh, crowning Empress Amy Freeman Lee, 1951.

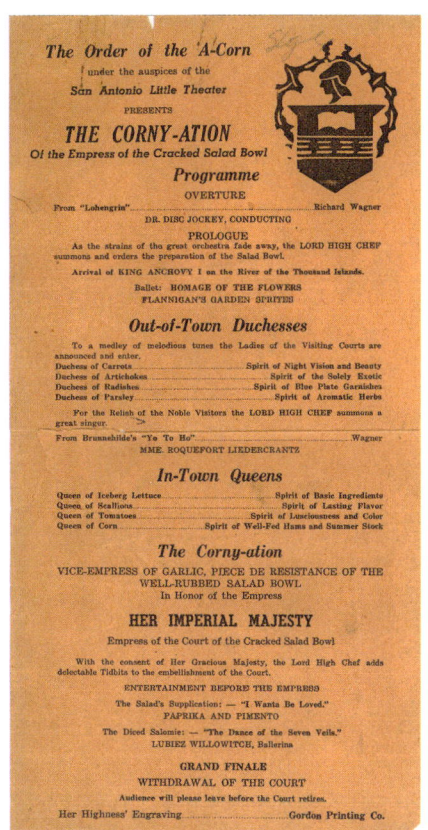

Program, 1951.

laughter. The royalty of this affair was businessman and building contractor Howard Bumbaugh, the venerable King Anchovy I. At the conclusion of the show, he crowned the "Empress of the Cracked Salad Bowl," Amy Freeman Lee, a visual artist and art critic.[2]

In the earliest years of Cornyation, the show satirized one of the oldest events in Fiesta San Antonio: the Coronation of the Queen of the Order of the Alamo. The coronation, an elaborately staged ceremony, presents twenty-four "duchesses"—debutantes in highly embellished gowns and trains who are to attend the newly crowned queen.[3] Cornyation, a satire of debutante pageantry, was developed at a moment when Fiesta was trying to expand and capture a broader public audience.[4] Cornyation presented itself as a show for the "little people" of the city while simultaneously advertising that it was organized and fashioned by sophisticated artists and designers. It was a show that both appealed to the common man (and woman) and included jokes for a cultured audience.[5] The event became so popular that it was parodied by other groups in the city and turned into a major fundraiser for SALT.

THE BEGINNING OF A LONG TRADITION

Cornyation was the brainchild of three men: Russell Rogers, Homer "Chips" Utley Jr., and Joseph "Joe" Salek. Russell Rogers was from an old-line ranching family that developed the Shavano Park community in northern Bexar County.[6] Rogers was heavily involved in the running of the San Antonio Little Theater (SALT), the most prominent theater group in the city; he also served as a producer and performer.[7] Rogers met Joe Salek while Salek was studying for his master's degree in drama at the University of North Carolina. There they performed together in the 1941 play *Patience* as part of the Carolina Playmakers.[8] After a suspension of SALT performances due to World War II, the postwar revival of SALT included searching for a new play director, and Rogers recommended Salek. Salek was in his late thirties when he moved to San Antonio in August 1949.[9] Although Salek was supposed to work in a temporary position as the director of SALT, he enjoyed San Antonio so much that he remained as director for thirty-two years. Former SALT members fondly described him as intelligent, sophisticated, and a well-rounded actor and director. One SALT member and Cornyation duchess remarked that Salek was a "character," with a flair for the dramatic. "One night, we were at a cast party," the duchess remembered, "and Joe had been to the symphony, and so he came late. He opened the door like this, so dramatic. And he had on this long black cape and a top hat." Salek and many other SALT members fit into a prominent arts community that mixed with high society. He socialized within a circle of artists and patrons, such as John Palmer Leeper, director of the McNay Art Museum in San Antonio. In 1954 Leeper met Salek at a cocktail party at the art museum, and, according to Leeper, they "hit it off marvelously." Leeper recalled that Salek "had one of the most beautiful voices

Joe Salek at home, 1950.

I've ever heard." Salek became close friends with Leeper and his wife, traveling internationally with Leeper every summer and naming Leeper the executor of his will.[10] Arts patrons from the time period said that Salek was widely accepted within the art and theater world and that it was common knowledge that he was attracted to other men. An intimate group of men and women from the arts community spent Thanksgiving and Christmas Eve alternating between Salek's apartment and Leeper's home.[11]

Shortly after Salek arrived in San Antonio, his first Fiesta experience inspired the creation of Cornyation. Salek later reminisced: "It all started under a tree on Madison Street in King William [a historic district], where I was living at that time. I had moved here to be the Director of San Antonio Little Theatre and it was my very first time to experience Fiesta week. I was trying to take in as much as I possibly could."[12] Salek attended the 1950 "Court of Islands"–themed

Coronation of the Queen of the Order of the Alamo, 1950.

Coronation. He may have attended to watch Barbara Seale, longtime SALT member, provide entertainment for the Coronation court with her performance of the song "Voodoo Fantasy."[13] The Coronation gowns, spectacle, and ritual inspired the beginnings of Cornyation. As Rogers recalled, Salek commented to him, "I would sure like to do a satire on that sometime."[14]

The opportunity quickly materialized. In 1950, SALT had just performed *Riverside Revels*, a Gay Nineties review, at a new Fiesta event, A Night in Old San Antonio (NIOSA). When the San Antonio Conservation Society (SACS) invited SALT to provide entertainment again during the 1951 Fiesta, the first Cornyation show was born. Salek directed and organized the show, but the first script was written by Rogers and his good friend and fellow SALT member Chips Utley.[15] Utley, a graduate of Abilene Christian College and a World War II veteran, had just moved to San Antonio to be a speech arts teacher at Alamo Heights High School.[16] In the first Cornyation, "with clumsy and humorous ceremony, her imperial majesty, Empress of the Cracked Salad Bowl, was crowned by King Anchovy I on the river of the thousand islands,"[17] spoofing the previous year's Court of Islands. Female members of SALT paraded down the steps of the bridge to the Arneson River Theatre's stage in colorful outfits. A review in the *San Antonio Light* proclaimed

Kay Crews as Her Asthmatic Majesty, Empress of the Court of Allergies, designed by Alan Cozby, 1952.

The Order of the A-Corn

Under the Auspices
of the
San Antonio Little Theatre
PRESENTS

The Court
of
Everlastin' Human Annoyances

PROLOGUE

As the STRAINS of the great orchestra fade, the LORD HIGH PILL PUSHER prescribes ELIXIRS, ANTIDOTES, and TRANQUILIZERS to soothe the vexation of the noble assemblage.

Arrival of KING ANCHOVY VII on the River of Damitol

The Royale Ballet Ache .... "Fit for a King"
The Colic Kids

Irksome Out-of-Town Duchesses

To an illegible prescription of highly recommended melodies and tunes, the Ladies from the Visiting Courts are announced and enter.

Encouraging Lousy House Keepers .... Duchess of Eternal Texas Dust
Recalling Pollen Packin' Mamas .... Duchess of Noxious Roadside Weeds
Glorifying der Gesundheit .... Duchess of Fussy Feathers
Suggesting the "Hair of the Dog" .... Duchess of Pink Elephants

For the Inoculation of the Noble Visitors, the Lord High Pill Pusher gives 'em the Needle.

From "Medic's Fiendish Delight" .... "I've Got You Under My Skin"
HYPO and DERMIC

Rash In-Town Queens

Starting from Scratch .... Queen of Poison Ivy
Symbolizing the Shot in Vein .... Queen of Vaccinations
Hatching Harassing Hives .... Queen of Berry Patches
Representing the Nicotine Fit (Filtered) .... Queen of Havana Stogies

The Corny-ation

HER DISTRAUGHT HIGHNESS, VICE-EMPRESS OF HAYFEVER, ASTHMA, and ALL ALLERGIES AND IRRITATIONS
To Distress the Empress

HER MISERABLE IMPERIAL MAJESTY

Empress of the Court of Everlastin' Human Annoyances

DIVERTISSEMENT FOR THE EMPRESS

"Malady in Blue" .... From "Lo-and-Groan"

MME. SALLI PATICA

THE GRAND FINALE

The Audience Will Pass Out Before The Court Expires

ENGRAVER TO THE EMPRESS .... Gordon Printing Co.

Program, 1957.

Fiesta for the Little People

8

that the Cornyation, "a clever takeoff on the fiesta's coronation," was the "talk of the evening."[18] Reviews commended Salek for the script and for his ad-libbing, and the female performers for their "rib-tickling performance."[19] There were hints of gender-subversive content in even this first show, during which "masculine mermaids . . . delighted the audience with their antics while reclining on the edge of the stage."[20] Little did Salek, Rogers, and Utley know that they had just created a smash hit, a show with enduring appeal that would be performed for another thirteen years and then be revived in the 1980s.

CORNYATION AND CORONATION

The Cornyation was a "merry travesty,"[21] a "glorified spoof,"[22] and an "annual burlesque"[23] of the Coronation of the Queen of the Order of the Alamo. One society column writer comparing the two events warned that "if you're a stranger in town, there's a difference between the two shows."[24] For the first decade, Cornyation operated in close relationship with the actual Coronation. Designers and scriptwriters created the themes, pageantry, and basic structure of the satire to directly mock the Coronation and elite culture more generally.

To fully understand the appeal of Cornyation, one must understand the role of the Coronation in 1950s San Antonio. In the 1950s Coronation was one of the major Fiesta events, and the most exclusive. In *Dressing Up Debutantes: Pageantry and Glitz in Texas*, anthropologist Michaele Thurgood Haynes notes that since the first coronation in 1909 the basic structure of the event has endured relatively unchanged. Each coronation is based upon a different theme and each year twenty-four young women of marriageable age process individually across the stage and up the stairs to appointed seats where they await the arrival of the princess and the crowning of the queen. The Lord High Chamberlain announces each young woman's name and title—titles such as the "Duchess of Scythian Antiquities of the Court of Fabergé" or the "Duchess of Symphonic Elegance of the Court of the Imperial Hapsburgs." The queen and princess bear equally hyperbolic titles. The Coronation is presented by the Order of the Alamo, a private men's club that was created by Virginian-turned-Texan John Carrington.[25] Carrington formed the club with the sole purpose of crowning a queen of San

Antonio, drawing on traditions of British aristocracy and southern chivalry. The club selects women from elite Anglo families to participate; thus, as Haynes suggests, the Coronation is an extension of Anglo elitism in San Antonio.[26]

The debutante pageant has always been presided over by King Antonio, who was the king of Fiesta and "host of the party" in the 1950s and 1960s.[27] King Antonio is selected from the Cavaliers, another exclusive, Anglo-dominated men's club in San Antonio founded shortly after the Order of the Alamo.[28] Just as seen with the royalty designated by many civic celebrations and Mardi Gras societies in the South, the king is a usually an older established businessman or professional, whereas the queen is young and unmarried.[29] King Antonio is a public figure during Fiesta, attending a range of public events and visiting schoolchildren. However, with the exception of appearing in the Battle of the Flowers parade, the queen's duties were mainly private until 1957, when she started to be included in public visits.[30] As Salek observed, the formality and exclusiveness of this event just begged to be satirized.

Cornyation wasn't the first event to poke fun at the Coronation and at elites. In the 1910s and 1920s burlesque parades and mock coronations were a common part of Fiesta. Burlesque was a theatrical parody linked to Victorian-era variety shows; the burlesque parades included floats of men mocking local and national politics. Middle-class members of the city often put on these mock coronations, which even in the early twentieth century included cross-dressing men (evidence of festivals' creation of a temporary space with different rules). In 1915 one float sported men mocking suffragettes as the "Suffer-yets," dressed in "hoop skirts, hobble skirts, jackets with balloon-shaped sleeves, headgear of antique design, and misfitting clothing."[31] When Queen Loco and King St. Vitus were crowned in 1917 in an "uproariously funny mock coronation held on Alamo Plaza," Rotary Club members Edward Raymond and Charles Fichtner played the mock royalty.[32] The next year some of San Antonio's most prominent citizens, including the famous San Antonio architect Atlee B. Ayres, performed a "Womanless Wedding," a "popular folk production and a farcical parody of a Protestant wedding ceremony" performed with a similar script in churches, public schools, and other venues across the country.[33] The men performing in the wedding often cross-dressed or wore blackface. In the 1918 Fiesta, the

Womanless Wedding, a fundraiser for war bonds, replaced the Coronation, which was cancelled due to World War I.[34] And in 1925 the Conopus Club sponsored a mock coronation at the Menger Hotel that featured both men and women as duchesses; Lady Richard of the House of Surkamp was Princess of the Rain Lilies and William C. King was a "blushing flower girl who danced before the royal court."[35] The performers in these early cases of Fiesta satire were frequently established middle-class businessmen, and the satire was rarely included in any systematic way in the festival.

A FIESTA FOR THE LITTLE PEOPLE

Cornyation was an important part of the growing inclusiveness of Fiesta in the 1950s. Laura Hernández-Ehrisman, in her history of Fiesta San Antonio, suggests that Fiesta in the 1950s included an "increasing emphasis on Fiesta as a mainstream, inclusive festival, a party for Everyman."[36] Some of this increasing emphasis resulted from a power struggle in the association that organized Fiesta as more middle-class businessmen without ties to the heritage elite organizations became involved in the association.[37] Reynolds Andricks, a civil engineer who was the leader of the Fiesta San Jacinto Association from 1950 to 1960, advocated most strongly for expanding Fiesta to include the Anglo middle class.[38] Fiesta organizers wanted to broaden the participation of San Antonio residents in the festival and used the language of democracy and inclusion so common in the postwar era to make this change happen.[39] This emphasis on broader participation was also a response to major demographic changes in the city. The 1950s were a time of dramatic urban growth in San Antonio; between 1940 and 1970, the population of the city doubled as it became the fifteenth-largest city in the country.[40] There was increasing economic pressure on Fiesta organizers to encourage Anglo middle-class residents to venture out of the northern San Antonio suburbs and into the downtown celebrations.[41]

Fiesta organizers created more opportunities for middle-class residents to take part in the festivities, including offering alternative royalty and new, more afford-able events. In 1948, Andricks masterminded a second major Fiesta parade, the "Fiesta Flambeau," an illuminated nighttime parade that featured floats from

11

Peggy Perron as the Duchess of Poultry, designed by Jess Bell; Mary Ellen Black as the Queen of Lightning Rods, designed by Eddie Hartman; and an unidentified duchess. Court of the Glorified Barnyard, 1955.

groups overlooked in the "day parade" or Battle of the Flowers parade.[42] In 1950 Andricks created a new member of the royalty, Miss Fiesta, as a scholarship pageant for deserving young middle-class women.[43] Another of the major new events that was affordable and accessible to middle-class residents was A Night in Old San Antonio.

Immediately after World War II, the only cheap and inclusive Fiesta events were the Battle of the Flowers parade and the Fiesta Carnival.[44] A Night in Old San Antonio changed that. The San Antonio Conservation Society (SACS) had begun NIOSA as the Indian Harvest Festival in 1936, and Fiesta organizers invited it to become a part of Fiesta in 1946.[45] Middle-class and upper-class Anglo women founded SACS in 1924 for philanthropy and for the preservation of the city's historic landmarks and cultural heritage.[46] SACS helped to restore one of the city's oldest neighborhoods, La Villita, in the heart of downtown San Antonio, a process that both preserved a Spanish heritage site and displaced Hispanic residents of the neighborhood. When the Indian Harvest Festival moved to La Villita in 1947 it was renamed A Night in Old San Antonio.[47] The event created tourist commodities out of different cultures by featuring food and music from American Indian, Spanish, and Mexican heritages, as well as the Old South and Gay Nineties.[48] In the 1950s NIOSA was widely attended by middle-class Anglo families, college students, and members of the military. Hernández-Ehrisman argues that NIOSA "demonstrated the gap between the romantic rhetoric of restoration and the reality of a racially stratified society."[49] SACS organizers positioned themselves as the experts on Mexican and other ethnic cultures yet relied on the labor of their Mexicana housekeepers to run the event.[50] As part of NIOSA, entertainment played at the Arneson River Theatre.[51] For fourteen years this entertainment was Cornyation.

Drawing on language of democracy and inclusiveness, SALT directors and scriptwriters quickly positioned Cornyation as a show for the common man, the "little people." The duchesses in the Cornyation were not the esteemed daughters of the Order of the Alamo, and the show was not presided over by King Antonio. Instead, the Order of the A-Corn, a mock organization of theater men, oversaw the affair, which was the antithesis of the Coronation: cheap, witty, loud, and appealing to the masses. The use of the words "corn" and "corny"

Nancy Hendrix as the Queen of Mascara, designed by Alan Cozby. Court of Cosmetic Subterfuge, 1953.

offered a critique of their own. The term "corny" had been popularized in the 1920s by jazz musicians to describe outdated music. [52] By the 1950s "corny" had come to mean old-fashioned, overly sentimental, or unsophisticated. In this way it positioned the Cornyation as a rustic, unsophisticated event in contrast to its elegant counterpart, but this may have been an indirect criticism of the Order of the Alamo or the Coronation itself for being old-fashioned or behind the times in a period of sweeping social change in San Antonio.

ESTEEMED KINGS AND EMPRESSES

Cornyation was an extension of Salek's basic philosophy of community theater, that it "should have as broad a base as possible, and should not only appeal to many different types of people . . . from many different walks of life and social strata . . . but should actually work those people into its program." [53] Cornyation included everyone from men as dress designers to women artists as queens to small children performing ballet as the entertainment.

Despite its appeal to the "little people," Cornyation still had ties to high society. Leeper and Rogers both were members of the Order of the Alamo and served as Lord High Chamberlain, the master of ceremonies of the Coronation. Several members of elite families, such as the Maverick family, or of the San Antonio Conservation Society were part of the show. [54] Coronation duchesses frequently attended Cornyation on Thursday evenings to see the show, and attendance at Cornyation was often reported in the social pages of the local newspapers in the 1950s. Despite this overlap, Cornyation remained a more middle- and lower-class affair.

Although the title of King Anchovy was created for the first Cornyation, fitting in with its theme of the Cracked Salad Bowl, the royal title stuck, and has remained through subsequent iterations of the show. This royal figure has typically been a middle-aged businessman like the first king, Howard Bumbaugh. Early Kings Anchovy included Maury Maverick Jr., son of the mayor and a prominent liberal state politician; [55] jeweler Barnett Shaw; [56] and Judge Charles Grace. [57] In addition to King Anchovy, Salek, Utley, or another SALT member performed as the master of ceremonies, narrating the show and announcing the duchesses.

Although there were several female "duchesses" and "queens" in the satirical show, there was only one "empress" and one "vice-empress." Often the empress was a member of SALT, but the show directors also selected women from outside the theater group—typically older, established women involved in the theater or art world.[58] Cornyation empresses were unconventional women for their time: visible in the public sphere through their work, acting, or activism. The first empress was Amy Freeman Lee, thirty-seven at the time, a well-known local artist and art critic for cultural events with a regular column in the *San Antonio Express-News*. A positive review of the first Cornyation in the *San Antonio Light* remarked at the cleverness of the show's script, and the humor of Empress Amy Freeman Lee, who ignored the entertainment playing out on stage on her behalf by reading the funny papers, filing her nails, and playing canasta.[59] Future Cornyation empresses would include other artists like Alice Naylor, who was an illustrator and teacher at the San Antonio Art Institute.[60] Prominent members of the theater world also appeared as the empress; these included SALT regular performers Barbara Seale, Mary Byall, and Kay Crews. In 1960, Ann Moursand, who had previously been a Miss Fiesta winner, reigned as the "Empress of the Court of Broken Traditions." In 1957 Wanda Graham Ford, the wife of famous southwestern architect O'Neil Ford and outgoing president of SACS that year, reigned as the "Empress of the Court of Everlastin' Human Annoyances." (She was also well-known for her activism against the building of the new San Antonio Expressway, which was captured by a *Life* photograph of her protesting in front of a bulldozer.)[61]

Some of the other female duchesses and queens were in their twenties and thirties; however, older women participated as well, and several of the duchesses were married. One duchess in the late 1950s recalled her youngest son coming to watch her in the Cornyation and hearing him call out, "Don't fall down the steps, Mommy!" as she began her descent down the Arneson River Theatre stairs. Based on interviews with almost a dozen duchesses, most were members of SALT or friends of the dress designers through social or work circles. Not all of the women were young, slender, and marriageable, a contrast to those who

1.

THE COURT OF COSMETIC SUBTERFUGE

1953

ENTRANCE of the LORD HIGH COSMETICIAN

PROLOGUE

Ladies and gentlemen, you are privileged this evening to witness something extraordinary!!......A conclave of Royalty and the **Crowning** of the EMPRESS OF THE COURT OF COSMETIC SUBTERFUGE....As Lord High Cosmetician, I shall guide you COSMETOLOGICALLY and shall be a bridge between illusion and fact.

Since the beginning of time, women have pursued ways to make themselves more attractive. The modern advertising media have capitalized on this search and run the Cosmetic Urge into a billion dollar industry. Competition is very keen. The **Royal** House that I represent, however, will be more than sensational!...... We have arranged to have the most Fabulously Beautiful Women in all of History to endorse our products.

Here......(indicating the stage)......across the canal from you, is the mystical isle where this will take place. Here is a realm beyond time and space where presently you will behold the beauty preparations that have forever been hidden and secret from mortal woman....in a regal conclave....and witness the obeisance of Historical Beauties to their Empress.

The time is now! The GLAMOUR GALS of History come forth!!

1. Enigmatic....Cleopatra

2. The exotic QUEEN OF SHEBA

3. Beautiful HELEN OF TROY (there's the face that launched
                                    a thousand ships)

4. Our own dear....POCOHANTUS, Mrs. John Smith (Is there a Cap-
                                    tain Smith in the house?)

5. The beguiling favorite...MADAME POMPADOUR

6. Napoleon's stunning...EMPRESS JOSEPHINE

7. The SEXational....MADAME DU BARRY

8. And captivating....JEZABEL

Script excerpt, 1953.

participated in the Coronation. Some duchesses were unconventional women for the time; they took leadership roles in SALT, were older, or were Jewish. A few duchesses were unmarried "spinsters" who were identified as potential lesbians by fellow participants.

Women were also involved in Cornyation as scriptwriters, directors, and comic relief. Close friends Yvonne Schlichenmaier and Squeaky McGill wrote the "Court of Entertainment" script in 1961.[62] The comical entertainment for the event's royalty included a children's dance troupe; occasionally SALT women or men also performed comical routines. In 1953 Kay Crews "appeared in a black tutu, red bloomers and red stockings to dance the 'pas de one.' . . . She wound up flat on her back on stage."[63]

SOPHISTICATED ARTISTIC MEN

Although in the early years two women designed dresses, including Maxine Wharton from Joske's department store downtown, most Cornyation designers were men who worked in the arts or style industries. Russell Hill Rogers noted that "costumes were designed by the leading San Antonio artists."[64] These artists were men in their thirties and forties who were often unmarried and worked in the art and design world as hairdressers, florists, visual artists, window decorators at department stores, or drama teachers at the high school or college level. Roy Shuptrine was involved in Cornyation throughout the 1950s as a designer and hairstylist; he had worked for Joske's in the 1940s and became well-known for his couture in the 1950s and 1960s.[65] Bob Winn was director of the San Antonio Art Institute, which was part of the growing McNay Art Museum; he designed for the show from 1951 to 1955. A group of Cornyation designers owned The Studio, an art studio that included visual artists like Lesle Larsson and Bob Brown. Some Cornyation creatives were dress designers. Les Wilk, one of the youngest Cornyation designers, was a senior at Trinity University when he designed a dress for the Queen of Cold Cream for the 1953 Cornyation. He went on to marry and became well known for his couture dresses, eventually serving as resident director of Texas Woman's University's Southwest Institute of Design.[66]

Designer Bob Winn assisting with a charity drive, 1950s. ▶

Designer P. J. Allen constructing a float for the Battle of the Flowers parade, April 1948.

Some of these designers did artistic work and costuming for other Fiesta events. A designer from the first Cornyation show, Phillip Jefferson "P.J." Allen, worked at Ann Lewis Fashions in the city. In the late 1940s he started designing parade floats for the Battle of the Flowers parade, which would later become his vocation.[67] Artist Bill Reily designed for Cornyation one year but was better known in San Antonio for his work designing scepters and crowns for the Coronation.[68]

A few of the designers were Latino men. Gabriel Alonzo was raised in San Antonio, served in World War II as a young man, and worked as a display artist at Sears and Roebuck.[69] He started designing for Cornyation in 1955 and designed dresses in at least eight shows. In 1959 Adolpho "Ally" Garza co-owned with fellow designer Ron Michael the short-lived Serene Void Coffee House on the edge of Travis Park in downtown San Antonio.[70] Their coffeehouse hosted cultural and art events, including performers from Mexico and Spain, but was not part of the growing beatnik scene.[71] Michael Gene David, a Cornyation designer during the late 1950s, was the child of immigrant parents from the Philippines and Mexico.[72] Other Latino men worked backstage as stage crew or were involved in the promotion of the show.

Fellow cast members often described the Cornyation designers as "sophisticated" men, reflecting their expertise in the arts and experience living in major cities. A few of the designers spent their entire lives in San Antonio or moved to the city from a rural Texas town, but most designers had lived in or regularly visited Los Angeles, New York City, or San Francisco. For example, P. J. Allen was born in Kyle, Texas, but he danced professionally in New York City as a young man. Later he moved back to live in his family home and work in San Antonio.[73] Bill Ramsey and Victor "Vic" Anthony, who designed the first Cornyation gowns in 1951, moved to New York City and Los Angeles respectively a few years later. Designer Jud D. Davis, described in his obituary as an "artist, florist, gourmet chef, caterer, singer, dancer, and fragrance expert extraordinaire," was born in San Antonio but left the city to serve as a soldier in World War II. He later worked in the theater industry in Boston and New York City but intermittently lived in San Antonio and Houston as well.[74] Social columns in the newspaper reported that other Cornyation designers traveled together frequently on summer vacations, taking international trips to art museums and driving trips across the United States.

The exposure of these designers to the professional art and theater world in major cities influenced Cornyation scripts, costuming, and aesthetics. Many Cornyation duchesses described the designers as a "worldly" and "sophisticated" group of men who influenced SALT. One duchess recalled:

And you know, in the early days of the San Antonio Little Theater, we had hairdressers that would come and do our hair before the productions. I mean, it was just like Broadway. I had a dresser, very spoiled. In hindsight, I'm sure it was because all of these guys were so sophisticated. They'd seen a lot of New York theater, they knew exactly what went on, and everybody has a dresser in New York. So they tried to create that, and they did. We used to have black tie opening nights. It was a big deal.

[Going to New York] there's a sophistication that you come back with. A lot of people go back and live there . . . what you get from living there is with you forever. And so that's where they got their sophistication. They were well-traveled before they ever started doing what they did.[75]

This sophistication was about money, time, and expertise. As most of the designers were unmarried and without children, they had experience living, working, and vacationing in major cities. They kept up on the latest Broadway shows, as reviewed in the society column of the papers and the scripts of Cornyation. Several Cornyation participants remarked that this sophistication infused even Cornyation, as its humor often relied on double entendre and obscure theater references that only the sophisticated audience member could fully appreciate. These participants suggested that the humor of Cornyation went "over the heads" of most audience members.

This sophistication was also marked as gay. In the 1950s and 1960s there were many coded ways of referring to gay men, whether by calling them "swishy," "temperamental," or "sophisticated."[76] To be swishy was to be a feminine man, but to be sophisticated was to be artistic.[77] Joe Salek was known throughout the art and theater scene in San Antonio as a homosexual or gay man. Although some of the men mentioned here may not have been gay men, as a group Cornyation designers definitely had a reputation as being "gay hairdressers" or "gay artists." In the 1950s it was not yet common for individuals to openly "come out" and speak about their sexuality to heterosexuals. The characteristics of their life history—unmarried middle-age men involved in the arts and artistic occupations—indicate some of the few ways gay men were visible during this time period.[78] Often "everyone knew" you were gay, but it was rarely spoken about. Many individuals I interviewed for this project remarked that Cornyation was a safe venue in which gay men could be themselves.

A few lesbians were involved in the show, and I interviewed two lesbians who played prominent roles in the 1950s and 1960s. The show did not have a reputation, however, for including lesbians, and lesbian involvement and contributions were largely invisible. In general, gay men, particularly those sophisticated men in this show, were much more prominent in the public sphere.

◀ *Unknown designer and duchess. Court of Hallucinations, 1954.*

These men's sophistication probably contributed to the humor of the show. In the show's early years the humor was witty and smart; later it became more vulgar and campy. Camp is a contradictory art form; it is at the same time a sophisticated form of humor in its use of double entendre and coded language but also democratic and common. Gay designers and scriptwriters could simultaneously satirize politics with this vulgar humor while relying upon the audience's appreciation of their sophisticated artistry. This artistry may have protected them from the social ridicule that was still commonly pointed at gay men in this time period.[79] During the 1950s gay men and lesbians were oppressed by anti-gay laws, the medical classification of homosexuality as a mental illness, and nationwide anxiety via "lavender panics" about homosexuality and communism.[80] There was limited positive gay visibility: representations of gay life were prohibited in the movies, and it was not until 1964 that a mainstream magazine, *Life*, published a positive article on gay life.[81] Yet Cornyation designers may have avoided censure and ridicule while simultaneously criticizing elite culture and, eventually, city politics.

THE COURT OF COSMETIC SUBTERFUGE

One of the ways that Cornyation blended sophistication with satire was in its mockery of Coronation themes, royalty names, and general pomp. One particular target of Cornyation was the Coronation "court." Each Coronation court had its own theme; these were typically themes related to fantasy, history, or high culture. In the 1930s and 1940s it was common for the court themes to reference other cultures or high culture—there were, for instance, the Court of Imperial Russia (1937), the Court of Italian Renaissance (1938), the Court of Empires (1948), and the Court of Music (1939). Other court themes in the 1940s included the Court of Honour (1946) as the first court after World War II, the Court of the Old South (1940), and the Court of Gaiety (1949).[82] These themes emphasized the Coronation participants' cultured nature, which Michaele Haynes describes as "a mythologized ethnic and class history that justifies the hierarchical positioning of Anglo participants."[83] By emphasizing the importance of high culture and romanticizing imperialism, the Coronation emphasized the powerful position of the elite in San Antonio.

Conversely, the Cornyation themes glorified the mundane and comic. The early Cornyation courts included the Court of the Cracked Salad Bowl (1951, 1956), Allergies (1952), Cosmetic Subterfuge (1953), Hallucinations (1954), Glorified Barnyard (1955), Human Annoyances (1957), and Outer Space (1958). By focusing on everyday themes such as barnyards, allergies, and annoyances, Cornyation starkly contrasted with the dignified nature of the Coronation. The Cornyation court themes also referenced contemporary women's issues, such as dieting (or, at least, the eating of salad) and wearing of cosmetics. The Court of Hallucinations mocked common psychological disorders at a time when most of these disorders were considered to apply mainly to women.[84]

Within the Coronation court, each duchess was named in accordance with the theme of the court. For example, when Joe Salek attended the Coronation's Court of Islands in 1950 there was a Duchess of the Canary Islands in the Spirit of Neptune's Pearls, and a Duchess of Hawaiian Islands in the Spirit of Flaming Hibiscus.[85] Most of the names of the duchesses were long and included colorful allusions to high culture. In 1951 the Court of the Cracked Salad Bowl was also organized around a series of women proceeding through the audience, each announced with formal names. In this case, the Duchesses of Parsley and Carrots performed with the Queens of Iceberg Lettuce and Corn. Later, court names became increasingly longer and more satirical, often with puns or wordplay embedded within them. The Court of Allergies (1952) included the Duchess of Household Dust and the Vice-Empress of Hayfever. The Court of Everlastin' Human Annoyances (1957) featured the Duchess of Pink Elephants, the Duchess of Noxious Roadside Weeds, and Her Miserable Imperial Majesty.[86]

The Court of the Glorified Barnyard in particular is an excellent example of the satire used in Cornyation. A newspaper reviewer commented that "satirically dubbed the Court of the Glorified Barnyard, players poked good-natured fun at the regal music, dress, and with tongue[s] tucked deep in cheek, the royal titles of the gala affair."[87] This good-natured, tongue-in-cheek fun included women prancing around the stage in flannel sheets and dowdy costumes. The program for the Prologue of the Glorified Barnyard noted, "As the strains of the great orchestra fade, the LORD HIGH AGRARIAN magnanimously summons the SHARECROPPERS to render homage to royalty."[88] Salek, the Lord High Agrarian, announced the

Members of the Court of the Glorified Barnyard, including (second from left) Empress Alice Naylor, 1955.

King Anchovy, who arrived via "Ye Old Irrigation Ditch," the San Antonio River next to the stage. He introduced the "country duchesses," which included, "representing the Horsey Set . . . the Duchess of Nags," who mocked high-society women. Salek explained how delightful and attractive each duchess was; the irony of talking about the Duchess of Swine and the Queen of Lightning Rods as delicate young ladies was part of the humor of the show. The finale was "her horrendous highness, vice-empress of scarecrows and guardian of the throne and yards" and of course "her corn-fed imperial majesty."[89] This theme was a not-so-gentle mocking of royalty that contrasted high society with the sharecroppers and the "corn-fed," stressing the poverty and rural nature of the "little people."

GOWNS AND CROWNS

At the center of both Coronation and Cornyation were the gowns. The elegant Coronation themes were reflected in the gowns, as the entire event centered on duchesses coming down the runway in their dresses and trains. According to Michaele Haynes, at the Coronation "the elaborately bejeweled gowns and trains can be compared to the costumes of the circus and Ice Capades in terms of the glitter and the flash of the fabrics and glass stones. They are comparable to costumes of grand opera and Renaissance theatre in terms of the countless yards of velvet brocades, laces and braids, and the care with which they are made."[90] A Coronation Mistress of Robes supervised the designing and sewing of each dress; each gown reflected the theme of the event, its duchess's title, and family imagery. In the 1950s the dresses featured a "fashionably tight bodice and extremely full skirt silhouette" with a lot of tulle and chiffon, with the train often an extension of the skirt rather than a separate piece.[91] The Coronation trains were critical for identity creation, as "more than just glitz; through embroidery and beading they symbolically represent the thematic models of attainment and beauty, the legacy of members of the elite."[92]

The Cornyation outfits artistically and directly satirized the grandeur and pretentiousness of Coronation gowns. The spontaneity and cheapness of many Cornyation gowns contrasted starkly with the elaborate affair of the Coronation. Salek, Rogers, and Utley often boasted in the local newspaper that the gowns for Cornyation were created on a budget of two dollars or less, which was one hundred times cheaper than most Coronation gowns.[93] In the earliest years designers made the Cornyation gowns in the hour before the show with materials from the SALT costume closet. Later, Duchess Allison Bergwin Fenton recalled rivalry between Cornyation designers in the 1960s over who could make the most elaborate designs.[94] Even in 1952 a commentator noted, "The script was as funny as last year's, but the costumes and some of the stage business leaned more to the esthetic side. Some of the costumes this year were elaborate and handsome."[95]

Designers often constructed the Cornyation gowns out of mundane objects and fabrics—with, as Rogers suggested, "whatever they could get their hands on."[96] According to SALT participant Kay Crews, the first Cornyation outfits were

Edith Speert as the Duchess of Kissproof Lipstick and Bernice Krula as the Queen of Mud Packs, both designed by John Hornung. Court of Cosmetic Subterfuge, 1953.

"designed by top San Antonio artists and manufactured (usually with staples and pins) from materials as nearly as possible like the thing represented."[97] Thus the Queen of Parsley had actual parsley in her outfit, and food items and miscellaneous items such as beer cans, poker chips, and cheese graters were made into outfits. For the Court of Allergies, the empress's train was "embellished with coffee cans, carrots, and an allergy cookbook, [and] was bordered with peanuts in the shell, which members of her entourage cracked and ate during the performance."[98] Photographs of duchesses from the 1953 Court of Cosmetic Subterfuge demonstrate that many outfits were comical and hastily put together out of everyday objects such as buckets, cardboard, cotton balls, and tinfoil. Edith Speert, the Duchess of Kissproof Lipstick, wore a tinfoil hat that resembled the tip of a lipstick. Nancy Hendrix, the Queen of Mascara, carried a large broom with "Maybelline" written on it. Newspaper coverage described Empress Anne Thompson in 1953 as wearing "an ensemble of trailing yellow tarleton and cellophane, and her panniered skirt held a built-in dressing table with jars and bottles balanced on top. She applied makeup as she advanced down the aisle."[99]

Anne Thompson as the Empress of the Court of Cosmetic Subterfuge, designed by P. J. Allen. 1953.

Sometimes these gowns included trains or heavy items. The trains for the empress and vice-empress were often comical. Barbara Seale sported a train one year that resembled a monster clinging onto her shoulders and dragging the ground behind her. At times these mundane items contributed weight to the costumes, which mocked the Coronation ritual of putting young women in gowns with heavy trains with large headpieces or scepters. In the first Cornyation, for instance, the Vice-Empress of Garlic, Mary Ellen Black, wore "an odiferous necklace of garlic weighing five pounds."[100]

The center of attention in the Coronation and Cornyation alike were duchesses proceeding down the runway, showing their dresses. At Cornyation, the duchesses and empresses made their way down the steep stairs at the Arneson River Theatre through an audience of drunken adults and laughing children. Designer Robert Cotham "Bob" Jolly reminisced on the years at the Arneson:

> Why people weren't killed back at the Arneson I don't know. I can't walk down the center stair of the Arneson in flats. . . . I'm terrified to go down there in moccasins, and the Cornyation queens came down there in *six inch heels*. . . . Not walking. Prancing, dancing, leaping. They always came from the back, came down the stairs, ran over the bridge real quick, and appeared on stage. Yup. How they did that I will never ever [know]. It scares me to death to walk down those steps.[101]

In many interviews with former Cornyation duchesses, these women remarked that they enjoyed coming down the stairs at the Arneson, that it made them feel as if they were debutantes or pageant contestants, with the eyes of hundreds of audience members upon them.

As the duchesses processed down the stairs of the Arneson, the master of ceremonies announced each by name and the theme she represented. The Coronation Lord High Chamberlain used a flowery and fancy explanation of each theme, and the script for the early years of the Cornyation carefully mocked the tone and presentation of the Coronation script. In the 1951 show, the master of ceremonies for Cornyation gave the official Latin name for each salad vegetable, offered suggestions for how to prepare the dish, and remarked on how each duchess was feisty, crisp, or attractive—just like her vegetable. In the first six years, Salek directed the show, and Rogers and Utley wrote the scripts. Their scripts consistently used the educational tone of the Coronation but mixed in jokes about the attractiveness and availability of the women, which mocked the elite pageantry as a presentation of marriageable young women.

The show intentionally demonstrated corny and campy qualities. Cornyation used elite, well-known individuals for comic relief. Cornyation designers took young, pretty women and made them unattractive in burlap sacks and large

Presenting ....THE DUCHESS OF PARSLEY

In the Spirit of.....AROMATIC HERBS

Represented by Her Grace...GRACE VIRGINIA HOWARD CARRAM

of the HOUSE OF DRURY

COSTUME:

Designer: BOB WINN

A European ammiaceous aromatic garden herb
(Petroselium hortense) whose leaves are used as
a garnish. Native of Southern Europe, and has been
planted in gardens since the time of Charlemagne.

To keep Parsley fresh.....place her in a closed
fruit jar in the refrigerator.   Best in the salad
bowl if tufts are pulled from the stems and chopped.
To do this gather firmly in the left hand...and cut
through it repeatedly with a knife...or scissors..
until it is very fine.

Script excerpt, 1951.

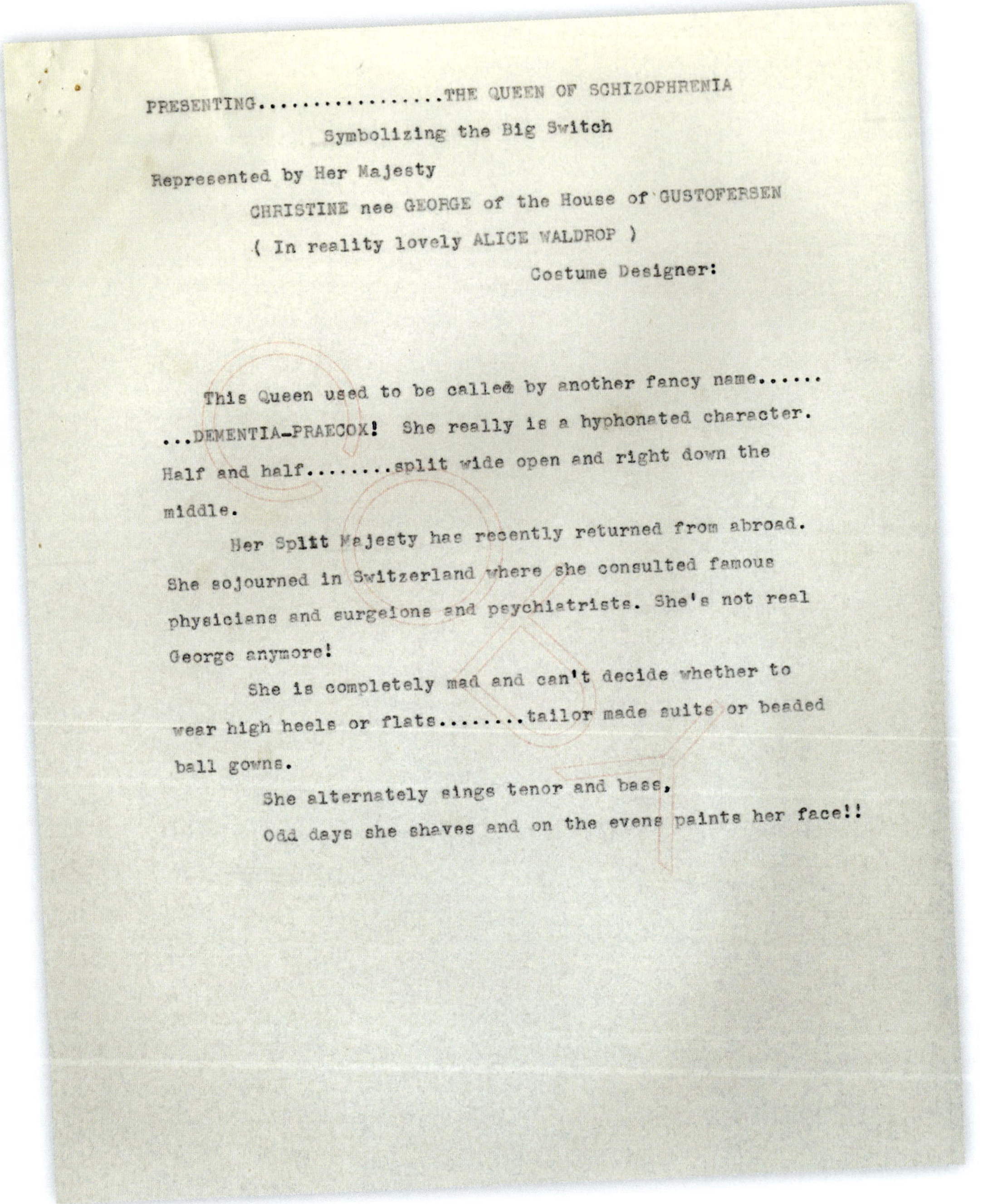

PRESENTING...................THE QUEEN OF SCHIZOPHRENIA

Symbolizing the Big Switch

Represented by Her Majesty

CHRISTINE nee GEORGE of the House of GUSTOFERSEN

(In reality lovely ALICE WALDROP)

Costume Designer:

This Queen used to be called by another fancy name......
...DEMENTIA-PRAECOX! She really is a hyphonated character.
Half and half........split wide open and right down the
middle.

Her Split Majesty has recently returned from abroad.
She sojourned in Switzerland where she consulted famous
physicians and surgeons and psychiatrists. She's not real
George anymore!

She is completely mad and can't decide whether to
wear high heels or flats........tailor made suits or beaded
ball gowns.

She alternately sings tenor and bass,
Odd days she shaves and on the evens paints her face!!

Script excerpt, 1954.

outfits, and by giving them messy hair or buck teeth. In 1954 the duchesses were described as "a group of local lovelies (hardly recognizable as such)."[102] Duchesses wore outfits that combined elaborate designs with found objects. Overweight or older women at times were turned into duchesses and queens, attended by a line of slave boys in skimpy attire. Well-known men in theater, business, and politics were transformed into King Anchovy, a laughable royalty. Profane items such as brooms for wands, fruit baskets for tiaras, and outhouses for a throne operated next to symbols of royalty and pageantry. In 1961 a review in the newspaper remarked that "the royal dresses are so bad that they're good. The empress' gown is a 'soft' combination of chartreuse fuscia [sic] and iridescent orange splotches on a black background. Put all the show's ingredients together and they spell corn—delightful, lavish, and well-planned corn, the secret potion of a successful Cornyation."[103] The show also worked in references to gay and lesbian culture, through nods to Greek culture or Alfred Kinsey. In 1954 one of the duchesses represented schizophrenia, and her outfit consisted of one half of a man's suit and one half of a dress, representing the "big switch"—this alluded to Christine Jorgenson's then recent, and public, sex transition.[104] These references were daring and indicated the gay artistry of the event.

"SPONTANEITY WILL BE THE SECRET OF OUR SUCCESS"

For SALT this yearly ritual of Fiesta irreverence quickly began to take on a character and purpose of its own. First and foremost, it developed a character of spontaneity. A memo to cast members from Rogers in 1952 included the admonition that "this satire is all in good fun. When a cast has a good time . . . the audience will too. . . . SPONTANEITY will be the secret of our success . . . certainly *not* rehearsal. The show should be funny, but in good taste."[105] According to a *San Antonio Express Magazine* reporter in 1953, the show is "a completely extroverted production where the cast has as much fun as the audience."[106] The show was not a polished and professional affair. Many duchesses reported drinking alcohol before or during the performance, which was the subject of much humorous reporting. In 1955 one reporter noted that "according to the program, 'the audience will pass out before the court retires.' At some moments it almost looks as if the audience will not have time to retire before the court passes out."[107]

1952

```
DICK CARR
JOE SALEK
JUD DAVIS
MODELS 1     5
       2     6
       3     7
       4     8
JIM MAVERICK
CEICIL FOX
SISSY PEYTON
MABEL McGEE
JACKIE FLANNIGAN
DOTTIE McCALL
NIKI WITTY
PAULA BUCHANAN
ELISE EVANS
EDWINA JOHNSON
PAT READY
LOUISE CLAIRMONT
KAY CREWS
BYRL TAYLOR
JOE CRUZ
ROGER READY
HAND MAIDEN
SLAVE GIRL
NUBIAN #1
    "   2
    "   3
ANN THOMPSON
BABA SEALE
CARL ATKINS
```

April 23, 1952

As you know, this satire is all in fun. When a cast has a good time....the audience will, too.

The entire profit from paid admissions to THE CORNY-ATION goes to the LITTLE THEATER BUILDING FUND. A $1000.00 or better deposit from tonite's efforts will certainly be a wonderful starter for a Campaign to get under way soon.

SPONTANEITY will be the secret of our success....certainly not rehearsal. The show should be funny, but in good taste. Each of you try to establish a definite personality (be it one that is simply carried away, demure, awkward, bored, dumb, or grand) but always one of dignity.

The program is the order of proceedure and the script in condensed form. By following it closely you should have no trouble. Here's to a lot of laughs and a good time had by all.

Russell Rogers

Chairman,
The Corny-ation Committee

Cast list and letter from Russell Rogers, 1952.

One element of unpredictability stemmed from the show's location at the Arneson River Theatre, in which audience members sat on an amphitheater of grassy seats divided from the small stage by a river. Female duchesses paraded down grassy stairs through the audience and across the river bridge, and the King Anchovy arrived in a boat or raft at the start of the show. Mishaps included performers getting stuck under the river bridge, having "wardrobe malfunctions" with cheap costumes falling off during the show, and falling into the river at the edge of the stage. King Anchovy Barnett Shaw fell into the San Antonio River during his reign.[108]

Cornyation performers recalled that this degree of fun and spontaneity carried over into their rehearsals. Cornyation rehearsals took over the Cos House near the Arneson River Theatre.[109] Many former duchesses and designers remembered how drunk and playful the Cornyation crew would become during the show. Former designer Roy Shuptrine remarked constantly in his interview just how much fun the Cornyation was for him as a young man, a hairdresser by trade, in San Antonio in the early 1950s.[110]

When Salek, Utley, and Rogers began Cornyation in 1951, they had no idea that they had created a new Fiesta tradition. But by the late 1950s Cornyation had become an enduring Fiesta tradition that fit into a long festival history of mocking elites. In the 1954 Cornyation, Barbara Seale commented, "You might say that Coronation is a take-off on ours."[111] Cornyation was also an integral part of the expansion of Fiesta. As an inexpensive, accessible event, Cornyation was enjoyed by people from across the city. It made Fiesta more even more inclusive by choosing as the focus of its satire the elite Coronation.

■ ■ ■

Welcome to the Court of Broken Traditions

The 1960s

The 1960s

The announcer enters the Cornyation stage to the music of *Fiorello!*, a Broadway musical about a New York City mayor who took on the political machine. Standing center stage, he introduces himself as a Gray Line bus driver who has been driving tourists around town. "You're about to see the *seamy* instead of the *sequin* side of San Antone," he proclaims, "things as they *really* are—the poor man's Cornyation . . . the Fiesta of the little people! After all, *this* is the 30 cent tour! Welcome to the Court of Broken Traditions. . . . You make 'em! We break 'em!"[1] And break them indeed they did. The King Anchovy that year, 1960, was visited by such luminaries as "Miss Chamberpot of Commerce, representing the tradition of progress" and "Miss Juvenile Delinquency, representing the tradition of Joie de Vivre." The Duchess of the Policemen's Ball mocked a San Antonio police scandal as "the favorite guest of all the police *men*," who "makes them forget duty toward crime and sin."[2] For San Antonio journalists, another duchess opined "all that's fittin' ain't necessarily in printin'" and proved that "the power of the pen is a helluva joke."[3] No one in the San Antonio political scene or among the social elites escaped mockery. The show even parodied feuds within the Fiesta Association regarding who was going to run Fiesta, including the demise of heritage elite control over the show. Mary Byall portrayed the "Duchess of the Spirit of the Fiesta Association, representing the tradition that a crushed spirit will rise again"; she sported a Confederate flag tucked into her dramatic hairdo.[4]

In the early 1960s Cornyation was more popular than it had ever been and repeatedly expanded, offering shows on more nights, with multiple performances per night, in order to accommodate its growing number of loyal audience members.

Program: The views you are about to hear do not necessarily reflect the opinions of the San Antonio Little Theatre

CORNYATION 1960

COURT OF BROKEN TRADITIONS – YOU MAKE 'EM, WE BREAK 'EM

(Siren sound, loud and piercing ... music to Fiorello ... Many uniformed police, much gilt, many badges and glitter; police running about, blowing whistles...etc.

Then, silence....

All lights on the narrator.)

Narrator is dressed in the uniform of a Greyline bus driver....he's bored and tired.)

NARRATOR: Evening folks. My name is Peachtree...That's right...Peachtree! I've been driving this sightseeing bus – The Turista Trotline – all over San Antone tonight and I'm plum wore out. And I reckon you tourists are tired of seeing so many ceremonies, coronations, presentations, misrepresentations, dancing brats, marching bands and such. So just sit down, rest your feet, kick off your shoes, loosen your collar, unzip your jackets, and make yourselves at home.

You're about to see the _seamy_ instead of the _sequin_ side of San Antone – things as they _really_ are – the poor man's cornyation....the Fiesta of the little people!

After all, _this_ is the 30 cent tour!

Welcome to the Court of Broken Traditions....

You Make 'Em! We Break 'Em!

But before the arrival of that lecherous old goat, King Anchovy X, let me introduce some real gentry....Queens and kings come and go, debutantes fade, but these really distinguished young ladies represent the cherished, sacred, _living_ traditions of the Alamo City. They are the bona fide traditions that can't be broken....They're always with us.

Our perpetual mistakes, the Queenlets of the 1959 Cornyation:

(Music: Rose of San Antone)

Miss Chughole, representing the tradition of transportation.

Miss Chamberpot of Commerce, representing the tradition of progress.

Miss Starling, representing the tradition of the nature of things.

Script excerpt, 1960.

Cornyation barker, unknown year.

High school students imitated the show at their fall festival, and lesbians and gay men playfully mocked the show in drag at a bar. Cast members' antics became increasingly brazen as the show began to satirize not just the debutante pageantry of the Coronation but also city and national politics. Cornyation during this period tried to show things "as they really are" on "the seamy side" of San Antonio. Costumes and humor became more campy and vulgar, to the delight of audiences and the dismay of the San Antonio Conservation Society. After attempts to censor the content and tenor of the show, in the winter of 1965 SACS disinvited Cornyation to Night in Old San Antonio. After one final show in 1965 at an Italian restaurant, Cornyation went dormant for more than a decade.

Unknown duchess. Court of Best of All Possible Worlds, 1964.

THE FASTEST-GROWING OLD SPANISH TRADITION IN LA VILLITA

In 1953 a barker for the show proclaimed to passersby that Cornyation was "the fastest-growing old Spanish tradition at La Villita."[5] The barker was simultaneously describing the newfound popularity of Cornyation and mocking the invented Spanish traditions at NIOSA. A review of Cornyation in the *San Antonio Express-News* that year proclaimed excitement over its new status as a regular show during Fiesta, a status gained by its popularity: more than two thousand people turned out to see the 1951 show.[6]

By 1953 Cornyation was the biggest draw in the Night in Old San Antonio midway, and by 1954 Cornyation appeared as an event in the guide to Fiesta in the *San Antonio Express-News*.[7] The show grew over the years to be offered two or three times a night for several nights during NIOSA. The shows were so popular that there were concerns over managing the foot traffic in and out of the event. By 1955 Cornyation drew just as many spectators as the Coronation. "This is not surprising," one journalist commented. "The Cornyation, started as a spur-of-the-moment gag four years ago, has rapidly grown into one of the durable traditions of the Fiesta San Jacinto. It is not meant for serious-minded people, and this is one of its greatest attractions."[8] In 1956 Gerald Ashford, regular columnist for the *San Antonio Express-News*, wrote an editorial suggesting that Cornyation had played a role in broadening participation in Fiesta. Ashford argued that Cornyation has grown into an "established institution."[9]

The show's growth in attendance and reputation benefited SALT. Although in 1951 SALT only netted a modest $217 from Cornyation, it quickly became a financially successful venture and SALT's largest annual fundraiser.[10] In 1964 SALT sold more than 8,500 tickets at 75 cents apiece, yielding a net profit of more than $4,700 (more than $34,000 in 2012 dollars). Cornyation funds helped to build dressing rooms and a scene shop, along with other renovations, in SALT's San Pedro Playhouse building.[11]

THE COURT OF OUTER SPACE

Part of Cornyation's increase in popularity could have been due to the new political focus of the show. Although Cornyation began as a satire of the heritage elite in San Antonio, by its 1960 Court of Broken Traditions the show had established itself as a critique of San Antonio life more broadly. The first sign of this shift was the 1958 Court of Outer Space, which mocked local social elites, including SACS. When the entertainment Sputnik and Explorer came in to dance, the emcee proclaimed the following:

> I'll have to ask the Constellation Society about your request to visit. . . .
> The Constellation Society says that there is no place for you to park. To make room, we would have to dig up our ancestral meteor park, in the center of outer space, and naturally, no one wants to desecrate our memorials, strange birds, and other characters that fill the park. . . . .
> The Constellation Society can give you a temporary parking permit, under certain conditions you can circulate in our galaxy as long as you don't conflict, adhere to the orbiting code, and for goodness sake, keep that dog from barking![12]

The Order of the A-Corn

Under the Auspices

of the

San Antonio Little Theatre

PRESENTS

The Court of Outer Space

(IT'S REAL GONE)

APRIL 22 - 23 - 24 - 25, 1958

PROLOGUE

As the STRAINS of the great orchestra fade, the LORD HIGH COMET magnanimously summons the Pleiades to render homage to royalty.

Arrival of KING ANCHOVY VIII on the Cosmic Stream

On the Edge of Outer Space .... "Les Rockets"
Missiles of the Dance

The Stellar Duchesses

Amid celestial strains, the Heavenly Bodies are announced and enter.

Representing High Skia Diving .... Duchess of Neptune
Representing a Heavenly Hot Dog .... Duchess of Pluto
Representing The New White Magic .... Duchess of Uranus
Representing Celestial Organizations .... Duchess of Saturn

Entertainment Before The Court

Ring Dem Bells .... Old Folk Song
Lilly Lakes

In Orbit Queens

Symbolizing Astronomical Figures .... Queen of Jupiter
Symbolizing the Wild Blue Yonder .... Queen of Mars
Symbolizing the Navigator's Delight .... Queen of Venus
Symbolizing a Flash in the Night .... Queen of Mercury

The Corny-ation

HER SUBLIME HIGHNESS, THE MOON, VICE-EMPRESS OF
OUTER SPACE, BACKING IN REFLECTED GLORY

In honor of the Empress

HER UNIVERSAL, INFINITE MAJESTY, THE SUN, EMPRESS OF
THE COURT OF OUTER SPACE

To bring to mind that all Heavenly Bodies are in
constant motion, the Lord High Comet presents:

JET STREAM .... National Dance
Three Little Aces

THE GRAND FINALE

The Audience Will Please Pass Out Before the Court Does

ENGRAVER TO THE EMPRESS .... Gordon Printing Co.

Program, 1958.

This script criticized SACS's approach to cultural conservation, which extended beyond the physical preservation of buildings to also include the regulation of how people interacted with cultural sites. What makes the 1958 show even more remarkable is that its scriptwriter, Chips Utley, also targeted the Cold War and the House Un-American Activities Committee, two much more treacherous targets. The show lampooned the race to space and the Soviet launching of Sputnik in 1957. It mocked the tension between the two major world powers. At the end of the show, the announcer proclaimed that the final royalty were empresses, not queens. "You will note that they are not called queens, for Sputnik is from a communist country, and Explorer is from a democracy which broke away from royalty, and wouldn't dream of crowning people king and queens, even in fun."[13]

Why did the show begin to change in the late 1950s? In 1958 longtime writer Russell Hill Rogers went on an extended trip to Italy, leaving Utley and other SALT members to write the script. After Utley moved to Turkey in 1960 to teach at an English-language school, other Cornyation participants wrote increasingly racy scripts. A scriptwriter from the early 1960s remembered in an interview that their initial attempt to make a "clean" script was altered by the Cornyation organizers to be more risqué, suggesting a broader commitment by the SALT board to pushing the edge. The show's changing content may also have been a response to the dramatic events of the 1960s, including the sexual revolution and the availability of birth control, the growth of social movements like the civil rights and student movements, and the Vietnam War. These events may have allowed for the exploration of more vulgar topics and a deeper criticism of the status quo.

During the 1960s the show still targeted high society and important organizations in town, including the Chamber of Commerce (the Chamberpot of Commerce), the Cavaliers (the Chevaliars), and the San Antonio Conservation Society (the Consternation Society). The show became increasingly focused, however, on city politics and critiques of city government. San Antonio politics were going through a phase of intense change as the city doubled in area during the 1950s.[14] This transformation led to far-reaching municipal reform in San Antonio with an emphasis on city services and efficiency. City politics quickly became controlled by the Good Government League, a political organization that was established in 1954 and dominated city elections between 1955 and

THE DUCHESS OF "SHOW ME THE WAY TO GO HOME"

REPRESENTING THE DISPUTED NORTHBOUND EXPRESSWAY

ONCE OUR DUCHESS WON A POPULARITY VOTE,

NOW SHE HAS POLITICIANS AT EACH OTHERS THROAT.

OUR LITTLE GIRL JUST CAN'T FIND HER PATH,

SHE ONLY SUCCEEDS IN STIRRING A STORM OF WRATH.

SHE KEEPS SEVERAL LAWYERS WITH LOTS OF PAY,

AND OVER HER FATE SOME ARE SAID EVEN TO PRAY.

HOLD ONTO YOUR HATS! YOUR BLACK HABITS! SHE'S GIVING IT THE GUN,

FOR OUR RADAR-RADIANT DUCHESS IS DETERMINED TO HAVE HER FUN.

THEY ARE STOCKING UP ON TRANQUILIZERS OVER AT THE ZOO,

AND THERE MAY BE SOME CONFUSION SEPARATING THE MONKEYS FROM THE DRIVERS WHEN SHE IS
                                                                                THROUGH.

THIS DUCHESS IS A MODERN WOMAN WHO'S HERE TO STAY,

EVEN THOUGH SHE MAY BE "COLLISION HAPPY" ON A RAINY DAY.

SHE'LL GIVE YOU A RIDE LIKE YOU'VE NEVER HAD,

HER USERS ARE GOOD, IT'S JUST THEIR DRIVING'S BAD.

I KNOW SOME OF US WILL LIVE TO SEE HER FINISHED,

THOUGH HOPE MUST OFTEN BE REPLENISHED.

HAIL TO THE MUCH DISPUTED DUCHESS OF THE NORTHBOUND EXPRESSWAY,

WHY DO YOU THINK KING ANCHOVY USES THE RIVER ANYWAY?

Script excerpt, 1963.

Unknown duchess. Court of Best of All Possible Worlds, 1964.

1971.[15] The early 1960s were also a time of contention in city politics, in which Chicano and black city council candidates began to challenge the hold of the Good Government League.[16] Most of the satire in Cornyation focused on city policies and scandals, including private city council "batroost" sessions that were not open to the public, and a police sex scandal. Other satires include critiques of how crime was being handled and of city services, via the crowning of queens of potholes, stoplights, and water services. Fiesta itself and the politics of who should run the festival became a source of inspiration for the 1962 Court of Fiesta Madness.[17]

Cornyation began to "tell the truth," participants claimed, about what was going on in San Antonio. According to Jim Collins, one of the show's designers in the 1960s and an audience member as a teenager, Cornyation revealed seriousness with humor:

> It was always very pertinent because, I mean, politicians are stupid now and they were stupid then. . . . Charlie Chaplin says that what

happens up close is tragedy but from a distance it's comedy. And that's the truth there. I mean, all these jerks pounding their chests and walking around, and then you have Cornyation that pointed a finger at the reality of what was going. I can't remember a specific script but I remember how funny it was because it was very pertinent and you knew what they were referring to.[18]

For Collins, Cornyation "pointed a finger at the reality of what was going on" and used humor to poke fun at politics and high society. In its campy humor the show demonstrated, as Philip Core argued in the 1980s, that "camp is a lie that tells the truth."[19] This camp demonstrates the way that satire and making fun can expose power dynamics and inequality to the audience.

THINGS GOT A LITTLE PURPLE

According to one former Cornyation duchess, "In the fifties, the Cornyation was witty. There was nothing dirty about it. Then as it went on . . . times changed too. In the sixties, we were in the middle of the sexual revolution. And so it got to be what it is now."[20] We usually think of the 1950s as a sedate period of time in American culture, when Cold War and postwar sensibilities kept the men at work, the women at home, and everyone in traditional gender roles. The conformity of the 1950s was bolstered by the House Un-American Activities Committee's very visible persecution of suspected communists; this persecution also targeted homosexuals, who were conflated with communists as risks to national security.[21] Yet, as Pete Daniels argues in *Lost Revolutions: The South in the 1950s*, this time period was one of vast social change throughout the South and Texas.[22] The widespread availability of automobiles and the growing influence of teenage culture made heterosexual courtship and dating more visible in public spaces; transgressive heterosexuals and homosexuals shared these public spaces.[23] The 1960s birthed the sexual revolution, with its increasing availability of contraceptives, rising rates of premarital sex, and "free love" culture.[24]

Although the early 1960s were relatively tame, Cornyation began to shift dramatically toward a more vulgar tone and humor. Bill Carter, who handled the music for the show, commented that in the 1960s "things got a little purple."[25]

The content, scriptwriting, and costuming of Cornyation became so racy that, starting in 1960, the emcee began to announce at the start of the show that "the views that you are about to hear do not necessarily reflect the opinions of the San Antonio Little Theater or any other self-respecting organization."[26]

Cornyation scriptwriters increasingly used double entendre to hint at growing norms of sexual exploration between men and women. This trend was exemplified by the 1958 Court of Outer Space (It's Real Gone), in which the emcee described the Duchess of Pluto as the "top dog of heaven," with references to hot dogs and male genitals; as she processed down the stairs, the emcee declared, "Wouldn't you relish this on your bun?"[27] For the Duchess of Uranus, the scriptwriters noted that "the stars are not really fixed but have motions of their own in the sky. Oh yes, I would like to say here, that our text is verified for authenticity by the *Encyclopedia Britannica*—A through Ass." This wordplay on the pronunciation of the word "Uranus" may have gone over the heads of some audience members, but it delighted others. The Duchess of Saturn "had a date the other night with a new fellow named Van Guard, but had to drop him as he was too interested in exploration."

Some of these references gestured toward gay life, gestures that may not have been comprehended by heterosexual audience members. The 1958 cast commented that for the Greeks, the Queen of Venus would have been known as the goddess of love, Aphrodite. "And who are we to contradict the Greeks?" they quipped. "Her period of rotation is not exactly known, but the Kinsey Foundation is working on it."[28] This description of the duchess hints simultaneously at the erotica of the Greeks and the Kinsey Foundation's books about male and female sexuality published in 1948 and 1953, respectively. Kinsey was most known for revealing high rates of same-sex sexual activity between men at this time. During the same show, scriptwriters made references to gay icons like Gina Lollobrigida and Sophie Tucker, the "last of the red hot mamas." In his study of pre–World War II gay life, historian George Chauncey describes how double entendre and coded language allowed gay men to "place themselves and to see themselves in the dominant culture, to read the culture against the grain in a way that made them more visible than they were supposed to be."[29] Cornyation

Aileen O'Callaghan as the Empress of the Court of the Sport of Sports: The Political Game in San Antonio, designed by John Angerstein, and King Anchovy Maury Maverick Jr., 1959. ▶

Elaine Honigblum as the Vice-Empress of Vice, designed by Gabriel Alonzo. Court of the Sport of Sports: The Political Game in San Antonio, 1959.

designers found a place for themselves within both Fiesta San Antonio and the dominant culture of social and political elites; their sophisticated satires rendered gay men "more visible than they were supposed to be" during the rapid social changes of the 1960s.

Beyond the scriptwriting and its topics, Cornyation's costuming also became more daring during this period. In the 1960 Court of Broken Traditions multiple queens wore outrageous costumes. The Queen of Conservation, mocking SACS, was a younger woman dressed with heavy face makeup, including dramatic bags under her eyes to insinuate her age, and layers of dramatic costume jewelry. Miss Red Light, a Duchess of Juvenile Delinquency, wore one of the most provocative outfits, between her decorated breasts and buttocks, her cigarette-filled hair, and her blacked-out teeth. One of the more remarkable trains was that worn by Elaine Honigblum, 1959's Vice-Empress of Vice. Her elaborate train included appliqued lettering of the words "Strip Poker," "Rape," "Guilty," and "Raid," along

◀ *Mary Byall as the Empress of the More-the-Marrier, designed by Roy Shuptrine. Court of Civil and Uncivil Projects, 1963.*

Unknown duchesses with Miss Red Light, 1960.

with several attached objects including girls' white underwear, money, playing cards, poker chips, guns, knives, sunglasses, and empty Lone Star beer cans that rattled as she came down the steps of the Arneson River Theatre. This costuming, coupled with the unpredictable frequency of wardrobe malfunctions on stage, made for a daring show indeed.

One of the most controversial performances of the show in the 1960s was that of the Empress of the More-the-Marrier of the 1963 Court of Civil and Uncivil Projects. The Empress Mary Byall spoofed the Kennedy family's prolific nature by parading down the Arneson Theatre stairs visibly pregnant and sporting a train with red-headed dolls on it. At the top of the stairs, Byall perched one baby doll on her shoulders as she called out, "Junior? Junior? Where are you?" To the amusement of the audience, she finally found the doll attached to herself and marched down the stairs dangling it by one arm.[30] The scriptwriter described Byall as a "lusty do it yourself beauty" who had "labored long and hard with a fantastic sense of duty." "She's against any kind of control," the script continued, "And those tax deductions will put Uncle Sam in the hole."[31] Byall not only broke social conventions about pregnant women being visible on the stage or screen; she did so while making witty jokes about contraception and childbirth.

IMITATION IS FLATTERY

Cornyation became so popular that it was imitated by at least two different groups—a club at a San Antonio high school, and a group of regulars at a gay and lesbian bar on the outskirts of town. These imitations show how ingrained the show was becoming in the public imagination of San Antonio residents.

For at least two years—1955 and 1959—the Gold Battalion club at Harlandale High School produced a Cornyation show of its own during the school's fall festival.[32] In the 1950s the high school hosted its own Coronation event for its students each fall, with courts like the Court of Holidays (1950) and students dressed up in fancy gowns and tuxedos. Harlandale's costumes were not as elaborate and as expensive as those in the real Coronation's, and its royalty selection process was more egalitarian; dukes and duchesses were elected from the ranks of the middle-class Anglo young men and women who attended the high school. It is unlikely than any of the young women were involved in the actual San Antonio Coronation event—thus the school's event may have been an opportunity for middle-class girls to debut. The Harlandale Cornyation was a satire of the annual school event and relied on the original Cornyation for its name, structure, and possibly content. The mock pageant included a Halloween theme one year. In photographs, the event appeared to be staged similarly to the Fiesta model, with a male master of ceremonies and a parade of female duchesses in comical outfits. That Cornyation was easily imitated by and recognizable to high school students, parents, and teachers suggests that it indeed had broad public appeal.

The G.B.'s presented the Cornyation at the Fall Festival.

Excerpt from the Harlandale High School Yearbook, 1959.

The show was also imitated by a very different group—members of the growing gay and lesbian world in San Antonio, in the first Cornyation drag show at a local bar. In the 1950s gay men and lesbians frequented a few bars in the downtown area, and a retired Air Force colonel, an Anglo gay man, opened the city's first exclusively gay bar, El Jardin, in 1954.[33] By the 1960s gay men and lesbians could frequent a handful of gay bars in town. Mary Ellen Mitchell, a heterosexual African American woman, owned a series of bars and establishments that catered to a lively mix of Anglo and African American straight and gay clientele.[34] Frequently, these bars were shared spaces between gay and straight clientele. For example, the glamorous Menger Hotel downtown included the historic Roosevelt Bar, where parade attendees met each other during the Fiesta, and which a group of older, sophisticated gay men frequented outside of the Fiesta.[35]

Many gay men and lesbians also went out into the country surrounding San Antonio to enjoy freedom and privacy.[36] Outside the northern city limits of San

Photo from Acme Bar, 1960s.

Antonio, gay men and lesbians frequented a bar nicknamed "the Country."[37] Anglo gay men and lesbians in the 1960s used the phrase as a code when they spoke to one another; in response to questions about where they were going for the evening they would respond, "Oh, we're going out to the Country."[38] To an outsider, this response sounded like a pleasant drive in the country; to the insider, it was a way of identifying like-minded individuals.[39] Although military police occasionally raided the Country looking for wayward soldiers, the rural setting was for the most part a welcome safe haven for drinking and dancing for the underground community.[40]

Anglo lesbian Carolyn Weathers wrote a short story, "Cheers Everybody," about pre-Stonewall San Antonio that highlights the growing visibility of gay men and lesbians in Fiesta. She tells witty stories about the River Parade, a night parade with floats built on riverboats that begins the festival. She remembers that "gay men waited on Fernando's patio to shout, 'Seafood! Seafood!' to the

Photo from the Top Hat bar, 1960s.

embarrassed sailors riding on the U.S. Navy float, while the sailors looked the other way and tried to pretend it wasn't happening, the same way they themselves yelled at embarrassed women in the streets who tried to act like they liked it."[41] In her slightly fictionalized account of Cornyation from the early 1960s, she recalls one of the duchesses being a gay man surreptitiously cross-dressing.[42] Weathers was not the first person to suggest to me that gay designers schemed to include secretive cross-dressing in the show. Although there is no evidence that this cross-dressing happened, the reports of scheming about such activities suggest that gay designers tested the boundaries of the show at this time.

Weathers remembers acting as the master of ceremonies at a drag show performed at the Paul's Grove Country bar on May 5, 1963, just after the regular Cornyation event. The drag show included some cast members of the real show and was viewed by regular bar attendees along with a few straight and prominent San Antonians who were associated with the NIOSA event. Weathers recollects that "it was a thunderous success. In my diary entry for that date I say the first show was great, and the second show was hysterical—and we were all potted (meaning half-lit with lots of Lone Star beer)."[43]

The Cornyation drag show included a few Cornyation duchesses, but it primarily starred duchesses who were men dressed in drag. The show mocked Fiesta by featuring duchesses of events like NIOSA and the Western Parade.[44] It also mocked Cornyation by listing a designer for each duchess and a fake organizational sponsor. These organizational sponsors included the "Downstairs Division of the Order of the Alamo Plaza," the "Upstairs Division of the Greyhound Bus Club," and "Local 69 of Streetwalkers International." One of the more explicit duchesses was sponsored by the "DoMore Cowboys."[45]

The script of the drag version of Cornyation modeled itself after the regular Cornyation's mocking of the Coronation, creating an exquisite blend of fashion commentary, camp, and vulgarity. As the Duchess of the Pilgrimage paraded in front of the audience, for instance, Weathers as emcee called out:

> Sad and mournful in her black robe and train, this duchess still manages to bring a small amount of . . . gaiety into her costume.
>
> Lovely brocaded flowers adorn her train of Neiman Marcus net.
>
> She looks so pious—but somehow a bit perverted, too! Wonder where she's going on *her* pilgrimage?[46]

The Pilgrimage to the Alamo was a solemn affair hosted by the Daughters of the Republic of Texas during Fiesta.[47] This duchess spoofed the seriousness of the traditionally solemn procession with innuendo about gaiety, fashion, and pilgrimages. Another participant, the Duchess of the Flambeau, mocked the excesses of royalty with reference to the illuminated night parade. Weathers announced:

> Our vivacious duchess is truly a sight to behold.
>
> Her train is many-splendored. Here is a work of art all in itself. Each precious triangle of Japanese silk was sewn on by ten blind monks over a period of two years.
>
> The volcano near the center is symbolic of her hot nature and her fame as an eruptress.
>
> Her headdress is created of spun glass spikes aglow with jewels.[48]

This Flambeau satire sexualized the parade with phallic images of eruption and heat. The narrative mocked the elitism of the Coronation directly with its emphasis on the craftsmanship of the elaborate train and headdress. The combination of these elements created a campy critique of the pageant and, more generally, Fiesta.

Like the regular show, the Cornyation drag show was a hysterically good time. The drag show also marked a critical moment in which San Antonio's gay and lesbian community claimed Cornyation as its own event—and used drag to do so. The drag show ultimately contributed to the demise of the original show in the 1960s, though, because it attracted the attention of SACS members who then saw a connection between the city's gay and lesbian community and Cornyation that they may not have been conscious of before.

THE CONSTERNATION OF THE CONSERVATION SOCIETY

By the early 1960s members of SACS were beginning to express concerns about the Cornyation performances—both the costumes and the content. According to Salek, "The Conservation Society got to a point where they asked to read the scripts before we presented them. I suppose they thought they had to censor them or something. We should have known that the end to our fun was in sight. I would have to leave town during Fiesta because I just didn't want to be there and get all that flak. It was crazy!"[49] One Cornyation duchess remembered that during their rehearsals Salek would say, "Oh, you can't do that; the Conservation Society would be screaming at you," to some of their more vulgar suggestions. SACS edited the scripts for content and language, but many double entendres and vulgarities escaped their censorship. SACS found it more challenging to control the designers' costumes, the ad-libbing on stage, and the unpredictable wardrobe malfunctions, such as the loss of a "glittered bikini" by a male attendant during one of the show's final performances.[50] Cornyation attempted to accommodate SACS, though, inviting several members of the Conservation Society to the dress rehearsal in 1964.[51]

On February 12, 1965, the chairs of the San Antonio Conservation Society— Lillian Maverick Padgitt and Nelle Weincek—wrote to Salek and insisted that it was time to "make a change in the type of entertainment that is presented in the Arneson River Theatre, and to have a production suitable for all age groups attending our 'Nights' during Fiesta Week."[52] Referring to discussions within SACS that had been going on "for several years," Padgitt and Weincek made their case against Cornyation with the argument that it was not suitable for children.

Welcome to the Court of Broken Traditions

Salek later recalled that the women had "called us obscene—not family entertainment."[53]

Soon after these objections were voiced, a flurry of letter writing and meetings followed, including one between SALT, the Fiesta Commission, and SACS. Local businessman and SALT supporter Gene Brown, in a letter to Salek, stated that "my first reaction is that they were perhaps getting a bit stuffy over some of the broad satire so hugely enjoyed by audiences" but went on to suggest that it would be a loss for SACS not to have Cornyation perform at the Arneson any longer, as Cornyation drew large audiences.[54] Brown suggested that the audience would follow Cornyation to a new venue, which could be more profitable for SALT. Letters of support for Cornyation came from the mayor of Terrill Hills, Harold M. Scherr, who argued that Cornyation "had become so deeply woven into

Joyce Lambrecht as the Queen of the Orange Festival, designed by Ray Chavez. Court of the Greater Society, 1965.

the fabric of our community life that your decision will deprive us and our out-of-town, out-of-state, and out-of-country friends of a truly delightful annual experience."[55] A letter from the SALT board written on Marion Koogler McNay Art Institute letterhead by Cornyation scriptwriter John Palmer Leeper and designer Bob Winn describes Cornyation as a "unique tradition" that has been "mutually profitable to both organizations."[56] The letter writers also appealed to SACS as a fellow civic organization with a relationship to SALT. "If the Conservation Society has serious grievances against the Cornyation, whether financial, aesthetic, or whatever, they have not been presented to this Board of Directors. We have had no opportunity to settle such differences amicably[;] indeed, the differences have never been spelled out to us."[57] SACS and SALT board members made a plan to meet and discuss the possibility of reversing the cancellation.

Conservation Society members were not prepared for the fact that the wild popularity of Cornyation made its cancellation a subject of public debate through editorials in local newspapers. The *San Antonio Express-News* editorial staff applauded the SACS decision to meet with SALT and criticized Cornyation: "Amid its rare flashes of humor was an abundance of slapstick boredom. There were also frequent lapses of good taste."[58] In contrast, almost a dozen letters to the editor contested the decision, and editorial columns of both major municipal newspapers opined about the outcome. SALT supporter Glenn Tucker wrote an open letter to SACS in the *San Antonio Express-News*:

> It has been said you consider the annual event has lost its "niftiness," and has grown rather "droopy." I'm sure you don't use those words, because Webster defines "nifty" as "clever" and "droopy" as "bent downward." After 15 years running, the Cornyation—whatever else it may or may not be—can certainly not be dismissed as either unclever or sagging. Foolish? Yes. Corny? Of course. Silly? You said it. Childish? It's a babe in arms.

> But isn't this Fiesta Week too? Isn't that what we want the town's people and tourists to feel, to see and to hear during that mad, gay week?[59] Don't we want everybody to let his hair down and kick up his heels and pour out from a spirit proud how great it is to be alive?[60]

In an open letter to SACS in the *Express-News*, Kenneth Maples argued that SACS members needed to broaden their minds and the organization's membership, that censorship efforts had unduly tamed the 1964 Cornyation, and that Cornyation "in its purest form is instructing satire."[61] That the show was becoming increasingly campy and brazen had a definite impact on SACS's decision, and after a February 1965 Conservation Society meeting, Cornyation was indefinitely kicked out of NIOSA. SACS members justified the decision with complaints about foot traffic in and out of the show and objections to the vulgar scripts and risqué costumes that made it impossible for Cornyation to be described as a "family show."[62]

YES, VIRGINIA, THERE WILL BE A CORNYATION

Despite these setbacks, Cornyation designers and producers, along with the SALT board, were determined to move the 1965 production forward. Scripts had already been written, and Fiesta was merely weeks away. The group scrambled to find a new location for the show, to put together advertising, and to solidify the script. The Cornyation board printed a bumper sticker ("Yes, Virginia, there will be a Cornyation") to proclaim its defiance of the SACS decision. SALT made arrangements to hold the show at Villa Fontana, a local Italian restaurant near La Villita. The San Antonio City Council (whose members were clearly fond of the show) made special provisions to allow Cornyation barkers to solicit passersby on the sidewalk outside the restaurant to encourage them to come inside and watch the show.[63] The Fiesta San Antonio Commission allowed SALT to become a participating member organization and for Cornyation to be an official event.[64]

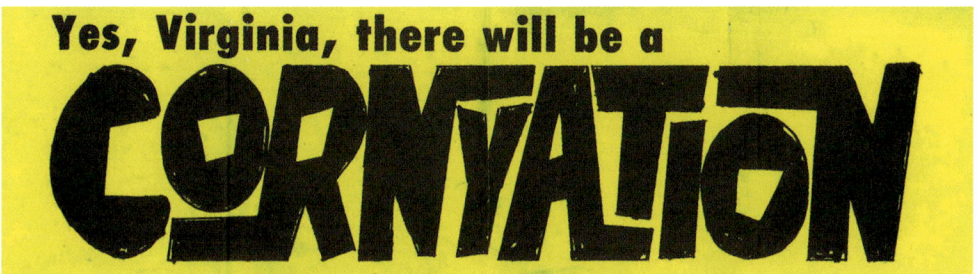

Yes, Virginia, there will be a CORNYATION

This show—what would be the final show for more than a decade—featured unrestrained camp and costuming. It mocked the festivals held by surrounding towns, such as the Cuero Turkey Trot and the Poteet Strawberry Festival. Humorous rhymes throughout poked fun at the sudden change of venue. The final original cast song, "Hello Anchovie," addressed to the "Kingie" Anchovy with a playful misspelling, included the lines "We're in a new location / And without provocation / We fell with the Alamo / What more to say / But we're moving

The Order of the A-Corn

Under the Auspices of the San Antonio Little Theatre

PRESENTS

The Fiesta Court of

THE GREATER SOCIETY

at the Villa Fontana Ballroom — 330 East Nueva
by two of the Poverty Stricken — Betty Jarman & Ted Fredricks
setting by William L. Ernst

April 19, 20, 21, 22, 23, 1965 at 8:00 & 10:00 P.M.

ARRIVAL OF KING ANCHOVY XV

Phil Ransopher .... Jim Collins, *designer*

abetted & assisted by CLOWN PRINCE O

Tommy Splittgerber .... Jim Collins, *designer*

to greet our mighty Monarch — 4 of the elite "400"

Mistress Sybil Rights .... Betty Lewis
Mistress Dagmar Dropout .... Shirley Boring
Mistress Penelope Peacecorps .... Kandee Kerr
Mistress Melanie Medicare .... Peggy McCreless

the "adora-belles" of the Greater Society
designer — Pete Martinez

SALUTE TO KING

HELLO ANCHOVY .... The Toast of the Town

Regal Visitors to the Court

Our visitors are not only out-of-town — but in-the-country

DUCHESS OF THE TURKEY TROT .... Audrey Davenport
She feathers her own nest   John Sharp, designer

DUCHESS OF WURST WEEK .... Peggy Trahan
A sausage every Sunday   Mike Estafan, designer

DUCHESS OF THE TOMATO FESTIVAL .... Billie Jean Ford
Please don't pinch   Gabriel Alonzo, designer

DUCHESS OF THE SPINACH FESTIVAL .... Cathy Brewer
A muscle in every can   Bob Jolly, designer

WAY OUT ENTERTAINMENT for way out visitors
Bonanza .... Phyllis Adler

THE IMPERIAL HOUSEHOLD

These Ladies just flew South for the Winter

QUEEN OF THE ORANGE FESTIVAL .... Joyce Lambrecht
A "sun-kist" beaut.   Ray Chavez, designer

QUEEN OF THE STRAWBERRY FESTIVAL .... Lillian Nixon
A tantalizing dessert dish   Grady Bryan, designer

QUEEN OF THE WATERMELON THUMP .... Joan Ottavio
She's ripe on the vine   Ramon Ramos, designer

QUEEN OF THE PEANUT FESTIVAL .... Patricia Bowling
She's a "real nut"   George Rosenkrans, designer

WESTERN BALLADE (Texas-Style)

THE GREAT SOCIETY . . Sadi Bug, Bobbie Hartlove & Kandee Kerr
Music, Lyrics & rights: Red River Dave

HER ICY VICE-EMPRESS, held together with Needles & Pins
She's the sewingest gal in town! .... Alice Vollmer
       Elden Stalnaker, designer

HER IMPERIAL BYRDSHIP — THE EMPRESS OF THE
COURT OF THE GREATER SOCIETY .... Bonnie Sheil
       Jesse Blair, designer

ENTERTAINMENT FOR THE BIRDS

Blue grass of Texas .... Kay Coleman

GRAND FINALE

Master of Ceremonies .... Jeffery Craggs
Master of Royal Robes .... Bob Brown
Court Musical Recordings .... Bill Carter's Record Rendezvous
       McCreless Shopping Center
Pages to the Court .... Sadie Perron, Kandee Kerr & Bobbie Hartlove
Production Manager .... Buddy Horton
Center of All Activity .... The Studio

Program, 1965.

King Anchovy Phil Ransopher, designed by Jim Collins, and Bonnie Shell as Her Imperial Byrdship, designed by Jesse Blair. Court of the Greater Society, 1965.

forward / With fair hearts stalwart and with the help of old Henry B / We're on our way Kingie to Hemisfair, Kingie."[65] Politician Henry B. Gonzalez, who would go on to be the first Latino mayor of San Antonio, was a firm advocate for HemisFair '68, the official World's Fair that would be held in San Antonio; the city's commitment to the fair entailed massive construction in the southeastern downtown area of the city, including the dislocation of residents through the acquisition of their houses via eminent domain.[66] The tone in 1965 was optimistic; the song lyrics suggest that SALT and the show were moving forward alongside the city's progress in creating the new Hemisfair Park.

Despite these efforts, the new version of Cornyation flopped. Given the dismal attendance and the fact that SALT barely made a profit, the board was forced to admit that holding the event independent of NIOSA was impossible.[67] For nearly two decades, the show lay dormant.

■■■

Revival in the Ballroom of the Bonham

the 1980s

the 1980s

On a humid April evening in 1985, on the top floor of the newly established Bonham Exchange, a disco bar in downtown San Antonio across the street from the Alamo, the ballroom is full of people. Cheering, raucous, and slightly drunk from their trip to NIOSA, the crowd goes wild when the show starts. The tiny ballroom in the bar includes a runway and tables, but people stand shoulder-to-shoulder and practically hang out of the open windows in order to see the stage. Fitting with the show's theme, "The Twelve Dames of Christmas," its announcer, Robert Cotham "Bob" Jolly, announces that the next duchess is "our Queen of Ruins, six geese a layin', representing the Conservation Society." The narrative parodied the recent relocation of the Fairmont Hotel building.[1] Earlier in April, the Fairmont Hotel, a structure built in 1906, had been moved at the behest of SACS from downtown to five blocks away in the La Villita Historic Arts District.[2] The hotel's slow movement from one part of downtown to the next made the Guinness Book of World Records as the largest structure ever moved on wheels.[3] At this, the 1985 edition of Cornyation, the Duchess of the Fairmont Hotel promenaded on roller skates, embedded within a huge hotel stand and garnished with a Fiesta hat. The crowd went wild as she proceeded down the small ballroom runway guided by a young man in construction gear with hard hat and boots.

Three years earlier, in 1982, Cornyation had been revived, rather inauspiciously. The Bonham Exchange ran a Fiesta ad announcing that there would be a 10 PM show on the Tuesday night of Fiesta that was "A Satire on Fiesta." Ray Chavez and Bob Jolly were at the helm of this cheap and campy ship. Both Chavez and

Duchess of the Fairmont Hotel, accompanied by Gregory McAlpine, 1985.

Jolly had been Cornyation designers in the early 1960s and remembered the show fondly. The ballroom of the newly established Bonham Exchange proved to be the perfect venue to bring the show back. The former designers revived a number of Cornyation's elements, including its focus on the gown and aesthetic of each duchess and the use of satire and campy humor to critique political events. Although the SALT board and directors were no longer at the helm of the show, Cornyation organizers contributed a few thousand dollars each year to the community theater from the event's proceeds.

The circumstances of the revival differed significantly from the show's debut in the 1950s. In its new home, where children were denied entry, the show could be as bawdy as it pleased, without facing regulation by SACS.

The national and municipal context had also changed. The gay and lesbian world of San Antonio had grown in visibility and strength; a local gay newspaper, the *Calendar*, covered the show, as did the citywide newspapers. Cornyation's revival also coincided with the beginning of the HIV/AIDS epidemic, which would change the nature of gay life for decades to come. Chavez and Jolly could not have guessed at the time that their Cornyation would go on to operate for more than three decades as an official Fiesta event and eventually become one of the largest HIV/AIDS fundraisers in the city.

THE GAP YEARS

After its last show at Villa Fontana in 1965 Cornyation was dead but not forgotten. Its spirit lived on in the minds and hearts of former designers, duchesses, and audience members. Although SACS had booted SALT and the Cornyation out of the Arneson River Theatre, the First Repertory Company of San Antonio often performed satires and comedy shows there during Fiesta in the 1970s. These shows included the Fiesta Nacho del Frio in 1974, complete with dancing nachos, a king, and a six-by-twelve-foot papier-mâché taco floating down the San Antonio River. Fiesta Nacho del Frio was directed by Wayne Elkins, who would go on to direct SALT and design for Cornyation in the 1980s.[4] Some gay men I interviewed for this project also remembered drag shows that mocked the Coronation being put on in gay and lesbian bars in the 1970s. Although not officially associated with Cornyation, all of these events were evocative of the show's satirical style and aesthetic.

After its 1965 demise four men remained interested in reviving Cornyation—Joe Salek, Jack Harmon, Bob Jolly, and Ray Chavez. In 1979 former designer and SALT director Jerry Pollack, hoping that Cornyation would again be a successful fundraiser for SALT, arranged to have Cornyation return to the Arneson River Theatre. Put on by Salek, Chavez, Jolly, and Harmon, the Court of Disco lampooned disco

DRAFT   ~~CORONATION~~ *Ozonation 79*

DISCO MUSIC UP AND BEHIND

CHANCELLOR ENTERS FROM SIDE.

June —
This is an update on the
Script! You will see the final
thing on Thursday. Smudgy Jay Pollick

CHANCELLOR: Fun Seekers, Society Ladies, Gentlemen, Tupperware
Party Hosts, Juveniles, Dogs, Scum of the earth perhaps; Welcome
to the disco that all America is waiting to get in! Like your
Doctors' Office - or Better yet like flying stand-by on Tejas
Airlines. I'm the very high - Lord Chancellor. So high I'm
always out of sight except during four nights of Fiesta. This
is the only and most exclusive disco in NIOSA which is probably
the least exclusive event of the Fiesta. I look out on this
great audience and I have only one question to ask - How in hell
did you chic people (Drippy) get past the doorman?

HE DOES A FEW STEPS AND THEN COMES BACK.

Is the press here? We had to guarantee the right amount of
surnames to get them here. Nobody would go to a disco if they
didn't have a chance to see their name or face in print. Yeah
man, there's Ron Jones of the Express News SA Magazine. Tonight
he's also shooting for an underground Murdoch version called
SA Vile.

Script excerpt, 1979.

The Bonham Exchange
and
The Order of the A-Corn
FOR THE BENEFIT OF THE SAN ANTONIO LITTLE THEATER
Present

The Court of Mythology

Arrival of King Anchovy XXIV
Thomas W. McKenzie

°ENTERTAINMENT FOR THE KING°
Ken Turner Productions

The Court

Representing the Tri-Party Safari
The Queen of the Amazing Amazons
Natasha Rep of the House of Tile
Designers: Bill Gage, Jim Whitaker

Representing the Alamo Dome
The Queen of the Elusive Utopian Unicorn
Catherine of the House of McNichol
and/or Michelle of the House of Moad-Hageman
Designer: Margaret Camp

Representing "The Last Temptation of Christ"
Queen Pandora & Her Box
Ana of the House of Van Vechten
Designer: Curt L. Slangal

Representing the Miller Lite Party
The Queen of the Bacchantes
George Ann of the House of Simpson
Designer: Pat Wells

°MORE ROYAL ENTERTAINMENT°
Ken Turner Productions

Representing the "Satanic Verses"
The Queen of the Fanatic Fatima
Stefania of the House of Baldesarelli
Designer: Amy Scheinman

Representing the Texas Academic Skills Program
Erato, the Queen of the Muses
Jae of the House of Berry
Designer: Chuck Ramirez - Hair: Fabian Garcia

Representing the Riverwalk Advisory Board
Queen Draco the Dragon
Susan of the House of Yerkes
Designer: Oscar Morales

Representing the Political Scene
The Queen of Medusa
Helen of the House of Dawkins
Designer: Robert Rosales

°STILL MORE ROYAL ENTERTAINMENT°
Ken Turner Productions & Molly Stevens/S.A.L.T.

Representing Ramses the Great & the Glories of Egypt
The Queen of Isis & the Vice Empress of Mythology
Julianne of the House of Rasmussen
Designers: Michael Bobo, Wayne Beers

Representing the Majestic Theater
The Empress of the Eternal Phoenix of the Court of Mythology
Gretchen of the House of Shoopman
Designer: Robert Rehm

°FINALLY THE FINALE°
Ken Turner Productions
The Ladies from S.A.L.T. • Kay Coleman, Molly Stevens, Jana Laven, Kelly Scharff

Script writter/Narrator: Bob Jolly
Director: Ray Chavez
Photographer: Mark Traeger
Program: THE LAZER'S EDGE
Crew: Patty "Faithful", Mark Porter, Thovas Brown, Robby Mahan, Greg Moczygemba,
Frank Marasco, Sharon Scott, Tommy Bundick, Dennis Sumner

Ken Turner Production Co. •John Vinton, Leonard Lopez, Cindy Cortez, Stacey Besch,
Stewart Scott, Corina Davis, Russell Fox, Ken Turner, Xavier Fernandez and Kurk Tibbles

---

Dedicated to the memory of Arthur P."Hap" Veltman, Jr.

Program, 1989.

culture, with a narrator posing as Elton John. The show was similar in form to the original Cornyation but with slightly more off-color jokes, including one about giving chromosome tests to the duchesses. The cast openly joked about the show's dismissal from NIOSA so many years prior, saying, "We'll libel anyone without fears / After the last Cornyation we were banned for fourteen years."[5]

The show did not attract a large audience, which made it less lively, less of a spectacle, and less lucrative as a fundraiser. Many SALT members at the time either did not remember the show or were unwilling to participate.[6] Although SACS had become co-ed and more diverse, the show still seemed too vulgar to be part of a family-friendly event like NIOSA. Clearly, Cornyation in its former form at the Arneson River Theatre was still not feasible.

A CHANGING CITY AND FIESTA

The successful revival of Cornyation as an independent show in 1982 was supported by changes within Fiesta San Antonio and, critically, by the creation of a new venue in downtown San Antonio.

Fiesta San Antonio in the 1980s was far less elitist than it had been in the 1950s. Although events like NIOSA and the Battle of the Flowers parade were still important, the festival had become a more diffuse "party with a purpose" focused on fundraising for nonprofit organizations. Since 1970, the festival had also become more diverse and inclusive of royalty outside the traditional social elites. When the League of United Latin American Citizens (LULAC) became a participating organization in Fiesta in the 1970s, its royalty, La Reina de la Feria de las Flores, became one of the sets of royalty that presided over Fiesta. Other female royalty that had been added to the event included the queen of the San Antonio Charro Association in the 1970s and, in 1969, the Queen of Soul, a queen for the city's African American community. These royalties also rode in the Battle of the Flowers parade and reigned over Fiesta. One of the biggest changes in Fiesta, though, was the addition of a new king to reign alongside King Antonio. In 1980 LULAC premiered Rey Feo (the Ugly King or People's King), a new royal figure who challenged the prominence of King Antonio.[7] Rey Feo

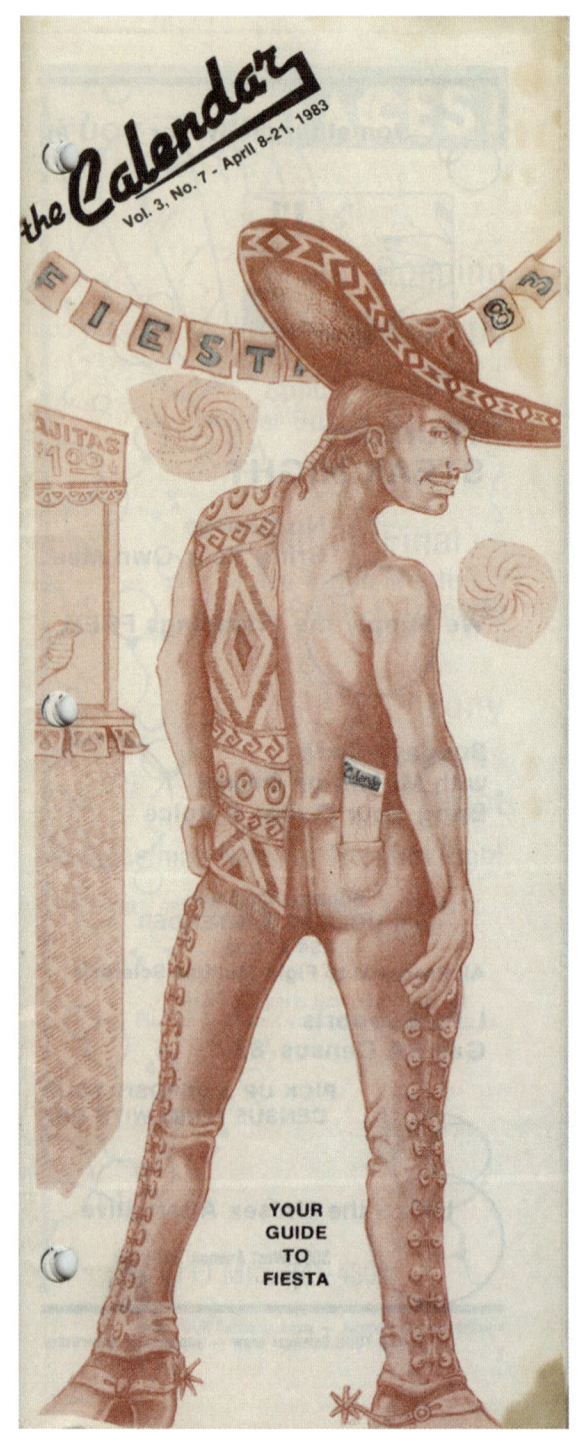

Cover of the Calendar, *1983.*

earned his position by raising the most money for LULAC's scholarship program. These changes in Fiesta reflected a larger shift in political power toward Hispanic and African American communities in San Antonio city politics; the grassroots-style barrio organization Communities Organized for Public Service (COPS) destabilized city politics in the 1970s and 1980s by bringing political attention to long-neglected, Hispanic-dominated west- and south-side neighborhoods.[8] In 1981 San Antonio voters elected Henry Cisneros as the first Hispanic mayor of a major U.S. city.[9] These social changes created space within Fiesta for groups from across the city to be included as an important part of the festival. And there was far less conflict over who was allowed in the event, as almost one hundred organizations participated.

The development of a stronger and more visible gay and lesbian (and, increasingly, bisexual and transgender) social world contributed to the creation of the Bonham Exchange, the new venue for Cornyation. Gay male designers of the 1980s inhabited a radically transformed social world compared to that of their 1960s counterparts. In the late 1960s the gay liberation movement emerged out of the Stonewall riots, a series of spontaneous, violent reactions to the police raid of a New York bar.[10] This movement included an emphasis on "coming out" and having pride in one's sexuality, allowing for record levels of gay and lesbian visibility in public.[11] This newfound liberation was not without resistance, though; the first national debate about gay rights revolved around a 1977 Dade County, Florida referendum on a municipal gay rights law that mobilized beauty queen Anita Bryant as its most vocal opponent.[12]

In the 1970s gay and lesbian bar life in San Antonio increased and became less secretive. Lollie Johnson, a San Antonio businesswoman, opened a series of bars targeting a lesbian clientele, beginning with the city's first lesbian bar, Hypothesis, in 1972.[13] There were multiple drag bars, including the Ponderosa in nearby Von Ormy, which attracted a lively Latino and black drag scene.[14] Future Cornyation designer and performer John McBurney cut his teeth at the Ponderosa as an artist, learning how to design hair, clothes, and makeup.[15]

One of the most significant changes in the decade was the establishment of the San Antonio Country, one of the largest gay clubs in the country, downtown by

The Ponderosa, 1971.

a group of men including gay entrepreneur and developer Arthur "Hap" Veltman Jr. Hap Veltman was a conservationist and developer in San Antonio; he led the development of the San Antonio River Walk and Blue Star Arts Complex, creating spaces for tourism and artistry in the city.[16] He named the San Antonio Country based on fond memories of the various bars that had been referred to as "the Country" in the 1960s and 1970s. The bar flourished as a multiroom space that welcomed everyone and was known for being a safe space for the LGBT community. It attracted a vibrant clientele, and its bartenders put on lively performances that were organized by Gene Elder, the manager of the club. When the bar ended up on the banned list of establishments for military members in the city due to its gay reputation, bar owners challenged this designation in military court.[17] Eventually Valero, a then-new natural gas corporation, bought the land on which the bar sat. Veltman used the funds from the sale to buy a historic building downtown, which he renovated into the Bonham Exchange. The multifloor, complex space turned into a premier destination for Texans who loved disco, dancing, and the open and inclusive character of the bar. In the 1980s gay and lesbian bars began to concentrate themselves north of downtown in an area that would later be called the Strip on Main Street.[18]

OLD DESIGNERS, A NEW LOCALE

Ray Chavez had worked with Gene Elder as a bartender at the San Antonio Country. When Chavez toured the new Bonham Exchange he was inspired by the room on the top floor, a ballroom with a small stage on which Cornyation could be performed. The three-hundred-person-capacity ballroom in the heart of downtown seemed the perfect place to revive the show. It was walking distance from NIOSA, so people could park downtown and attend both events. Veltman tolerated having Cornyation held at the Bonham Exchange during the festival as long as the event did not turn into a drag show, as Veltman disliked drag shows at the club.[19] Chavez called Bob Jolly, with whom he had been friends since the late 1950s, and suggested that they revive the show. Jolly joked that he had been thinking about the show and already had a script written, then enthusiastically developed a script that used the humorous rhyming style so common to the 1960s Cornyation scripts. This witty text became the 1982 Court of the Zodiac. The show featured such memorable royalty as the Queen of the Leather Scene, the Vice-Empress of the Moral Majority, and the Queen of the Fading Jet Setters. Jolly's script included satires of culture, social elites, and national politics.

The new Cornyation combined old and new faces. Some designers and duchesses had been involved in the 1960s version of the show, so audience members could still watch former duchesses Mary Byall, Joyce Lambrecht, and Kay Hamilton cavort on stage. Jolly served double and often triple duty as a designer, emcee, and scriptwriter. Designers John Shown, Chavez, and Jolly, veterans of the 1960s, were joined by a group of new young male designers and a few women. Shown was known in the art world of the 1980s for his stitchery wall-hangings, and he chronicled the happenings of the city's art scene in his magazine *Forum*.[20] Chavez was born and raised in San Antonio and could draw on expansive social networks as an artist, SALT member, and former San Antonio Country bartender. He drew on this pool of contacts to recruit designers and artists like Robert Rehm, Sterling Houston, and Brad Braune. Sterling Houston was an African American playwright, actor, and artist who had just moved back to his hometown of San Antonio after working in the art and theater world in Los Angeles, New York, and San Francisco.[21] Most of the designers were Anglo

and Latino men but in 1989 Pat Wells joined the Cornyation crew and would become a longtime Cornyation designer. She would be followed by other female designers in the 1990s and 2000s. Just as in the 1950s, many of the designers for the show were Anglo or Latino gay men, although a few lesbian designers would join the crew over the next decades.

As with previous Cornyations, the show featured people from across the city as duchesses, performers, and royalty. In the first show the local newspaper reported that "Star King Anchovy managed to miss event" due to imbibing too much.[22] Physician Earl Stenger, lawyer Ronald P. "Rusty" Guyer, and even Elder himself later made their debuts as King Anchovy. The role of empress also became less specialized; eventually she became just one of the duchesses who regularly appeared in the show and who was chosen as the last and final act of the night. Designers recruited their own duchesses from their personal social networks, often through connections in the theater world.

THE DUCHESS OF SAFE SEX

There were many similarities between the Cornyation of the 1960s and that of the 1980s. Most notably, the show still mocked elite culture, city politics, and national issues. The 1982 Court of the Zodiac included making fun of "kangaroo courts" and police speed traps along with elites (the "horsey set") and elections ("the political bull"), the surgeon general's report on cigarettes, the Fiesta Flambeau parade, and Hemisfair Park politics. Many of the designers were visual artists, and, according to one former designer, "it was pushy and edgy because everybody was artists so their instincts were to be edgy and push a lot."[23]

The 1980s editions of Cornyation targeted local politicians and city institutions, often satirizing evidence of fraud or mismanagement. In 1987 Sandra Castellanos represented local politics as the Queen of Sunday in the Park with Bernie, parodying the musical *Sunday in the Park with George* for the Court of Broadway Musicals That Never Were.[24] In her role, the *Express-News* reported, Castellanos appeared "carrying enormous scales of justice encrusted with scores of smoldering cigarette butts, [sporting] an enormous Mexican sombrero decorated

◄ *Anne Alexander as the Queen of the Social Lions, designed by Brad Braune. Court of the Zodiac, 1982.*   **77**

Duchesses watch the show. Court of Mythology, 1989.

as 'the Wheel of Politics.' Divided into pie-segments, the wheel encompassed Power, Fraud and Lies among the fortunes of civic duty." Castellanos's train, created out of Astroturf, read "Bernie: R.I.P.," reflecting the crushing electoral defeat of longtime city councilman Bernardo Eureste over a scandal involving the SeaWorld theme park.[25] The emcee's introduction of Castellanos lamented the mismanagement of local politics by the entire city council:

> *From the Halls of Magdalena's / To the shores of River Bend*
> *Our next old broad is famous / For amusement without end*
> *For she comes here representing / What our politicians do*
> *And with foibles unrelenting / Like a monkey in the zoo*
> *Be it Bernie's alterations / With no work permit in sight[26]*
> *Or Foxy Lou's vacations / That bring us all delight*
> *And of course there is Yolanda / With some she's quite a hit*
> *But the smokers are not fond-a / Miss Yolanda not a bit[27]*

And there's always Henry C. / With his dreams of greater glory[28]
One Election Day may see / Another ending to that story
The police still need a chief / And the firemen need a friend
And everyone's a thief / At least that seems the trend
C. A. Stubbs is still agog[29] */ And good old Weir Labatt*[30]
Once bitten by a dog / Now had trouble with a cat[31]

As was typical of other Cornyation skits, this duchess systematically targeted individual city council members and their foibles, including thievery, accusations, and grandiose aspirations. Among others, scriptwriter Jolly mentions Henry Cisneros, the first Latino mayor of the city. Fiesta as an event was still worthy of mockery, too. An announcement of the 1983 Cornyation court in the *Artists Alliance Review* paper noted that "Her Royal Highness, the Empress Turkey Divine, will reign over the Court of Haute Cuisine in the Grand Ballroom of the Bonham Exchange. Her Royal Highness will represent the San Antonio Festival and will be attended by the Vice-Empress, Apple Pie Alamo, representing the San Antonio Conservation Society, and King Anchovy, representing a mild aftertaste."[32] When former mayor Lila Cockrell took over Cisneros's position after she left office in 1989, the Court of Mythology represented Cockrell as Medusa, a spider with a web and hair full of snakes.[33] "Our last little queen / Can give you the shakes," the announcer stated, "For she comes to the scene / With a head full of snakes / For she represents / Political wrangles / And hers is a web / Full of snarls and of tangles."[34] The show also covered other controversies, such as the attempt to establish a shirts-off bar called the Naked Iguana on the family-friendly and touristy River Walk downtown.

The show also lampooned national events; income tax reform, presidential politics, the postal service, evangelical Christians, and television evangelists were all fair game. When Jimmy Swaggart was implicated in a sex scandal involving a prostitute, the show mocked the televangelist with the Queen of Press Your Luck. Scriptwriter Jolly quipped at the end of the skit, "But still there is hope / For the pure and the moral / For the favored position / Is still held by oral."[35]

A lot of attention in the show was devoted to the rise and demise of arts and cultural organizations, with particular attention to those pertaining to theater.

```
IN THE LIFE OF THIS OLD SCRIBE    THERE'S A QUESTION I MUST POSE

FOR HOW DO I DESCRIBE    AN IGUANA WITH NO CLOTHES

FOR YOU SEE THE FINE COMMISSION    OF OUR CHARMING RIVERFRONT

AS PART OF ITS TOUGH MISSION    HAD THIS PROBLEM TO CONFRONT

FOR A REPTILE IN THE BUFF    HAS TRIED TO SET UP SHOP

WHEN DO WE CRY "ENOUGH    THIS MADNESS HAS TO STOP"

I THINK I'M LIBERATED    AND I'M SURELY NOT A PRUDE

I CAN HANDLE THINGS X-RATED    BUT A LIZZARD IN THE NUDE?

WE THOUGHT WE'D SEEN THE END    TO THE NAMES THAT MADE US
                                                      SICK
WHEN THE BARGE WENT ROUND THE BEND    WITH THE BAR CALLED
                                                   BWANA DIK
YET DRAGONS SUCH AS WE    CAN SURELY FIND ANOTHER

WAY TO VENT OUR GLEE    THAN DEFILE OUR LITTLE BROTHER

AT THE RISK OF SURE PERDITION    FOR JUST THIS SINGLE TIME

I'LL GO AGAINST TRADITION    AND BREAK INTO MY RHYME

     Ann Maria Watson of the River Walk Advisory Commission
     has been quoted as saying "while I am a very liberal
     person generally, Naked Iguana just doesn't sound very
     much like the San Antonio River Walk that we all know
     and love."

SO LET'S GUZZLE DOWN SOME BEERS    AND GO DOWN ON A BANANA

AS WE GIVE THREE HEARTY CHEERS    FOR OUR NAKED IGUANA


REPRESENTING THE RIVERWALK ADVISORY COMMISSION

QUEEN DRACO THE DRAGON


_____ OF THE HOUSE OF _____


DESIGNER: _____
```

Script excerpt, 1989.

Sandra Castellanos as Queen of Sundays with Bernie, designed by David Sprinkles.
Court of Broadway Musicals That Never Were, 1987. ▶

Gretchen Shoopman as Empress of the Eternal Phoenix, designed by Robert Rehm. Court of Mythology, 1989.

Cornyation designer Robert Rehm became acclaimed for two related dress designs he made referencing the Majestic Theatre, a major theater downtown that was remodeled between 1987 and 1989. The 1987 Empress of the Song of No Way, Gretchen Shoopman, portrayed the decline of the Majestic Theatre for the Court of Broadway Musicals That Never Were. Two years later, in 1989, Rehm created another Majestic design, which was one of the most fantastic Cornyation costumes to date: a dress resembling a huge phoenix decorated with the magnificent arches of the Majestic Theatre. The same duchess, Gretchen Shoopman, portrayed the Empress of the Eternal Phoenix of the Court of Mythology. Her elaborate headdress represented one of the theater boxes.

◀ *Gretchen Shoopman as Empress of the Song of No Way, designed by Robert Rehm. Court of Broadway Musicals That Never Were, 1987.*

H. M. Jeanie Pancakes as Queen of the Leather Scene, designed by John Shown. Accompanied by Sterling Houston and John Dimler. Court of the Zodiac, 1982.

While the costuming and pageantry of Cornyation in the 1980s paid homage to the show's past, a changed aspect of the show was that gay issues and references to gay culture could be articulated in new ways that were not possible earlier. Because the show was housed in a rowdy adults-only bar, both scripts and performances became less coded and implicit and more bawdy and explicit. In 1982 this new aesthetic premiered with the Queen of the Leather Scene, who was attired in a leather dress and accompanied by two escorts, one of whom was designer Sterling Houston. Her outfit referenced the growth of leather fashion and community in gay culture, along with the gay liberation afforded by the sexual freedom of the 1970s. Other issues of concern to the gay community that would be represented by duchesses during the 1980s included the Moral Majority and, eventually, HIV/AIDS.

In 1982 AIDS had just recently been recognized as a disease that had already spread throughout the United States; throughout the decade it would become clear that many gay men were infected with HIV. The virus and its resulting disease were largely unknown while Cornyation was being revived. Although AIDS is now largely manageable through medication, the disease was a guaranteed quick and painful death sentence for more than a decade after its discovery in 1981. Over the course of that decade, HIV infected more than 100,000 people in the United States and became the number one cause of death for men between the ages of twenty-five and forty-four.[36] The disease ravaged the gay community and also the arts and theater communities in many cities. According to designer Brad Braune, "The notion of it was too frightening to make fun of or even acknowledge at all."[37] Cornyation acknowledged the growing epidemic for the first time in the 1987 Court of Broadway Musicals That Never Were with the Queen of the Sound of Mucus, Representing Safe Sex.

Even with the new permissiveness of the show, double entendre was still liberally infused throughout the script. Former director Joe Salek got in on the act, delivering an introduction at Cornyation's 1984 Academy of Surplus Awards with his friend and cohost Debbie Maltz.

> Joe: Well, here we are, Debbie, Cornyation night at the Bonham Exchange. Did you ever think you would be surrounded by so much royalty?
> Debbie: (startled look at Joe) I think there are more *queens* in the audience than there are backstage.
> Joe: I really don't mind bowing to royalty; it's when they ask me to get on my knees that I draw the line.
> Debbie: Oh those court bows! Well, it's OK; it's Fiesta week. Joe, have you ever been to the other coronation?
> Joe: You are putting me on! There's another one of these?
> Debbie: Yes, and the Order of the Alamo dresses are so heavy, that the duchesses have to practice by dragging blankets around after them.
> Joe: I don't know about blankets, but I've had plenty of practice dragging . . .
> Debbie: Maybe we better get started with the first award.[38]

At the start of the show that year, Bob Jolly proclaimed, "We have more sequins and feathers backstage than La Cage Aux Folles . . . and that's what the BOYS are wearing! Wait till you see what the girls have on . . . or don't have on."[39] In addition

the **Calendar**

VOLUME 5 NUMBER 9
MAY 11-25, 1984

MAGAZINE ABOUT TOWN

FIESTA AFTERMATH ISSUE

Cover of the Calendar, *1984.*

to the scantily clad women, men also began to appear more on stage, scantily clothed and in clothing that resonated with gay culture at the time, including cowboy hats, jock straps, and construction gear. This aesthetic extended to the entertainment; in 1983 "the not-so-royal court was entertained by 'Mona Enchilada and the Taco Revue,' a campy take-off of Les Ballets Trockaderos, an all-male ballet corps."[40] For 1989 King Anchovy Tom McKenzie, the permissive venue made for a wild three nights of the show: "When I was on stage was the

Designer Brad Braune and King Anchovy Tom McKenzie at the King William Parade, 1989. ▶

first time Brad [Braune] sent out a female stripper and every time she brought me something to drink she was wearing less and less, until she was wearing virtually nothing at the end. And then the next night was a reverse, and they sent a guy out. He was wearing less and less until he had a G-string at the end. On the third night I was like, 'What's going to happen now? How are they going to get to me this time?'"[41]

The revival shows built on other aspects of the earlier iteration of Cornyation, as well. The combination of genuine artistry and cheap, spontaneously created, campy outfits was a critical part of what made Cornyation what it is. The issue or satire was still represented in the costume of the duchess in question. In the early years of the revived Cornyation costumes were made quickly, often within less than three days of the show. In fact, designers recalled that initially they would learn about the theme for their duchess twenty-four hours before the dress rehearsal. In keeping with the Cornyation tradition, these costumes were often made out of everyday objects like trash bags, crepe paper, plastic dishes, Mylar, shredded paper, aluminum foil, and cellophane. According to one designer, "Part of the challenge back then was to see how cheaply you could do it."[42] The costumes quickly became more intricate, as designers gave more attention to detail due to the close proximity of the audience. Many duchesses sported long trains or heavy headpieces, maintaining the connection between the Cornyation and Coronation. According to one designer, the "idea was to give these girls horrible things, outrageous contraptions to drag around, which was the humor of making fun of the Coronation."[43]

AN INTIMATE AFFAIR

The audience experience of Cornyation in the 1980s was dramatically different due to the intimacy of the Bonham setting. The lack of a significant backstage and the use of a runway that went down the middle of the ballroom created an intimate connection between the performers and the audience members, who crammed into the room to see the show. When visual artist Curt Slangal attended his first Cornyation at the Bonham Exchange, he instantly wanted to be involved in the show. "My mind just went berserk because actually it was so

Unknown duchess. Court of the Twelve Dames of Christmas, 1985.

intimate," he recalled. "They had tables, round tables, and the bar with the little lava lamp. . . . It was just like a little romantic restaurant, and then everybody else had to stand. There was no A/C—the windows were all open. It was hot in there. But it was just, wow, crazy, and it was just such an earth-shattering thing for me . . . being from a creative background."[44] Many designers who participated during the decade remarked at how rowdy and participatory the audience was.

The 1980s revival of Cornyation was a much smaller affair than the shows that now draw huge audiences at the Empire Theatre, and many former attendees of the show at the Bonham express nostalgia for the intimacy there. For a few years in the '80s, the show was wild. Although the event was publicly advertised, one audience member said it had "more of an underground sort of feel." According to a Cornyation designer at the time, the crowd was "sort of the inner circle of people, arts community, the gay community, political people . . . it wasn't particularly a gay crowd, it was just sort of an insider crowd." This "insider crowd" was diverse and local. A newspaper review of the opening night in 1982 commented that "the 246-plus audience read like an Alamo City's Who's Who. Former debutantes, members of the San Antonio Conservation Society and businessmen were among those creating a standing-room-only crowd in one of the city's newest gay bars for the 45-minute spoof which has become a Fiesta tradition."[45] In 1983 one journalist remarked that Cornyation was already becoming "the place to be during Fiesta."[46] The SACS president attended in 1984. Tourists stuck out like sore thumbs, including one couple described by *San Antonio Express-News* columnist and Cornyation queen Susan Yerkes:

> Poor out-of-towners! One couple, here for an auto-dealers meeting, stopped in at Cornyation on the recommendation of a businesswoman the wife met in the Fairmount Hotel. Never has such a preppy-looking pair (she in pearls and silk, he in Gucci loafers and horn-rims) strayed into Cornyation territory. They were game about the gamey show, but when it ended, the fella was clearly shaken. "They're not going to believe this back in Kansas," he mumbled. But they were actually from upstate New York. We call that Cornyation-induced confusion.[47]

Although it was hard to get some social elites to attend due to the venue being a gay bar, these tourists were just one example of the diverse crowd drawn by the show.

BECOMING OFFICIAL

Although it was performed in an unusual venue, Cornyation as a show became more visible in the larger festival. Cast members marched in the King William Parade, a loosely organized neighborhood parade on the last Saturday of Fiesta. The King William Parade was sandwiched between two other major parades— the Battle of the Flowers and Fiesta Flambeau. Increasingly, official Fiesta royalty, namely Rey Feo and King Antonio, began to attend Cornyation as part of their official agenda, and members of the Fiesta Commission attended as well.

H. M. Yvonne Wood as Queen of the Horsey Set, designed by Leon Bridges and company. Court of the Zodiac, 1982.

Cornyation regained its status as an official Fiesta event, recognized by the Fiesta Commission, in 1985.[48] Cornyation's history in the 1950s and 1960s and the revival's association with Hap Veltman and the Bonham Exchange may have facilitated its recognition. Although dozens of events take place during the festival, the Fiesta Commission only recognizes, regulates, and promotes a select number of these. In anticipation of the first Fiesta-sanctioned Cornyation show, Veltman penned a letter to the Fiesta Commission in December 1981 proclaiming that the show "would be in keeping with the spirit of San Antonio Fiesta" due to its volunteer cast and its donating its proceeds to SALT. He recalled the long history of Cornyation being a part of NIOSA and opined that "the staging of this community-wide event, in the Grand Ballroom of this National Historic Landmark, would be a successful method of reviving this satire on San Antonio."[49] The letter casually mentioned that SACS would be having its own award ceremony in the ballroom as well. Within a month the Fiesta Commission replied that they had accepted SALT as a participating member organization of the Fiesta Commission. The commission declared that "your event is a welcome addition to our list and helps us represent virtually every sector of San Antonio's citizenry as participants in our annual April festival."[50]

Even as Cornyation was (re)gaining more popularity, its royalty, King Anchovy, was being afforded growing respect in the pantheon of Fiesta royalty. The traditional Fiesta royalty were officially established in 1980 by a Fiesta Commission rule that also barred any new applicants.[51] Cornyation created two royalty figures, however, who would become recognized as unofficial royalty by the commission in the 1990s. The first was King Anchovy; the second was the "Fiesta Hat King," who was born in the hubbub of the Bonham ballroom. In 1986, Cal Sumner, a regular Cornyation attendee with his brother Dennis and one who helped pass out programs, decided to distinguish himself from the crowd.

Cal Sumner at Cornyation, Fiesta 1987.

He appropriated an old theater derby hat and bedazzled it with rhinestones from various grand dames in his family. He wore the hat in front of the show's entrance, handing out programs and welcoming everyone with the phrase "Cornyation menu? Good taste not included."[52] Sumner collected bits of feather boa and costuming left behind by performers in the ballroom and added them to the hat. Each year he would add a few more pieces of ephemera, and his ever-growing hat became part of the Cornyation scene until he and his brother left the show in 1991.[53] Later, the Fiesta hat would grow huge, multilayered, built up over the years until it was more than three feet tall. Although Fiesta attendees often wore sombreros and other headwear, Sumner's hat inspired a new Fiesta style—the grandiose, creative, multilayered hat creation. In the 1990s Cal was designated the Hat King of San Antonio and recognized as unofficial royalty in 1998 by the Fiesta Commission, along with King Anchovy.

Cal Sumner, the Hat King, in 2003.

The decade that drew to a close with Cornyation royalty welcomed—if unofficially—into Fiesta was marked not only with a continuation of outrageous humor but also with incredible sadness. Cornyation was revived just as the gay community was facing one of its largest crises, the beginning of the HIV/AIDS epidemic. Little did the designers know that Cornyation would grow in future years to become one of the largest HIV/AIDS-related fundraisers in the city. Although AIDS was mostly ignored in the early years of the show's revival, by the late 1980s the epidemic was starting to affect the show. By the end of the decade, it had become increasingly common for shows to be dedicated to the memory of a dead cast member.

In 1989 this included a memoriam to Hap Veltman, owner of the Bonham Exchange, who had died at the age of fifty-two from lymphatic cancer, a result of HIV/AIDS, the previous December.[54] The 1989 Cornyation program—for the last show to be performed in the hot, rowdy, crowded upstairs ballroom of the Bonham Exchange—fittingly memorialized him.

It was clear by the end of the 1980s that Cornyation was outgrowing its home. A fire station across the street from the Bonham Exchange brought the attention of the fire marshal to the show, which often crammed two to three times more people into the ballroom than its maximum capacity. Fortunately, Cornyation had grown large enough to support a move to another major theater in town, the Beethoven Hall in Hemisfair Park.

■ ■ ■

Let the Queens Be Unleashed

The 1990s

The 1990s

Bob Jolly, longtime Cornyation designer and scriptwriter, warms up the audience in his new position as show emcee at Beethoven Hall, the new home of Cornyation, in Hemisfair Park. The theater, with its expansive stage and large runway, was for years the home of the Coronation.[1] Jolly disregards this history, though, as he announces the 1990 Court of Courts, a celebration of the twenty-fifth year of Cornyation. He starts the show by proclaiming that "the very first Cornyation assaulted the earth at the Arneson River Theatre in 1951, when the Court of the Cracked Salad Bowl was unleashed upon an unsuspecting public."[2] The 1990 show includes duchesses revived from past shows in the 1980s and the 1960s. Jolly announces the Queen of Pandora and Her Boom Box, in honor of the 1989 Court of Mythology:

> Stuff cotton in your ears / And greet this little fox
> For who not reappears / But "Pandora and her box"
> "Mythology" was her court / Her year was Eighty-nine
> Now she's back to man the fort / And she's feelin' pretty fine
> But Pandora and her BOOM Box / Is her altered appellation
> And from River Walk to boondocks / She's an ongoing frustration
> She's a fugitive from justice / For it's loudness that she sells
> She assaults our ears with gusto / With her hellish decibels
> But she'd best beware of strangers / With a penchant to detect
> For we have a fleet of rangers / And their meters are erect
> From the strip that's on St. Mary's / To the dirty nelly pub
> From a bar that's full of fairies / They are checking on you, bub

Ann Kinser as Queen of Pandora and Her Boom Box, designed by Curt Slangal. Court of Silver Splendor, the Court of Courts, 1990.

Even Santa and his Ho-Hos / Has got to keep it down
Bands of course are No-Nos / Even choirs can cause a frown
Now Pandora makes it clear / That to clean up the whole scene
Just relax and grab a beer / And move Taddy to Seguin[3]

With his intro, Jolly simultaneously mocked the efforts of longtime downtown resident Taddy McAllister, who had led a campaign to control the noise on the River Walk, and the continuing regulation of gay bars and public parks by the military police and park rangers.[4] The audience gasped as one of the largest Cornyation costumes to date, designed by Curt Slangal, was paraded onstage, showcased by smoke, strobe lights, and two dancers grooving to "Love Shack" by the B-52s. Standing on a fifteen-foot-tall platform with a skirt, the queen, Ann Kinser, teetered. As if the spectacle were not already grand enough, she revealed fold-out wings and a hidden panel at the base of her costume filled with scantily clad blow-up dolls.

Kimberley Corbin as Queen of the Not So Grand Canal, designed by Robert Rehm. Court of Silver Splendor, the Court of Courts, 1990.

The 1990 Court of Courts continued with designer Brad Braune's duchess, whose getup mocked the brewing national controversy over funding for gay and lesbian art at the National Endowment for the Arts (NEA).[5] Braune's queen wore chains and a headpiece shaped like a cage with floor-length silver streamers. Her black-costumed attendant was dressed as Senator Jesse Helms, who was leading the charge against the NEA.[6] Designer Robert Rehm then unloosed a repeat of the 1963 Court of Civil and Uncivil Projects with his Queen of the Not So Grand Canal. Out rolled Kimberley Corbin as a San Antonio River tourist barge. Her headpiece, a six-foot-long reproduction of a River Walk bridge, included twinkling lights, stuffed flying grackles, and camera-toting *Simpsons* characters posed like tourists.

Not only had Cornyation moved from the tiny ballroom of the Bonham Exchange to a major theater, but—for the first time—a Cornyation designer had secured corporate sponsorship to fund the costs of designing a costume. Curt Slangal had solicited funds from multiple local businesses to finance his design.[7] Sponsorship would become an increasingly common practice in the 1990s as designers used corporate funding to purchase materials and costumes for their duchesses. By 1999 more than half of all the designers had corporate, business, or individual sponsorships of some kind. Most of these businesses were small and local, including the Bonham Exchange and the On Main Card Shop. This funding and the larger size of the stage and offstage area of Beethoven Hall led to some of the most spectacular large-scale Cornyation designs ever built. Cornyation was becoming bigger, taller, louder, and prouder.

The increasing impact of HIV/AIDS on the city also transformed the event. The 1990 program dedicated the show to Wayne Elkins, a former SALT director who died at the age of thirty-seven after an extended bout with AIDS-related complications.[8] Although previous programs had included a memorial to individuals with AIDS, after 1990 almost every program for the next decade included a memorial or dedication to men who had passed away. The HIV/AIDS epidemic had hit San Antonio full force. Directors Chavez and Jolly made the decision to discontinue having the show serve as a fundraiser for SALT and instead registered the name of the show themselves and used it as a fundraiser for various charities, including many devoted to the care of adults and children with HIV/AIDS. This marked the beginning of Cornyation's transformation into a major fundraiser for HIV/AIDS.

LET THE QUEENS BE UNLEASHED

The audience flows into Beethoven Hall carrying not just your typical cascarones—the confetti-filled eggs that proliferate during Fiesta—but also bags of flour tortillas, beach balls, and bubbles. Before the show begins, audience members enthusiastically hurl flour tortillas at each other. Some of them have kept the bags open for a day or two to make the tortillas stale and easier to throw.[9] As the house lights go down, the audience is already wired. They go wild as the masters of ceremonies, Bob Jolly and Marina Pincus, come on stage to begin the show. To celebrate the end of each duchess's promenade across

Ann Kinser as the Empress of Fiesta 100 and designer Curt Slangal. Court of Outrageous Pretentiousness, 1991.

the stage, audience members throw tortillas, which are quickly swept up by the broom boy and girl, part of the stage crew.[10]

Why are Cornyation fans throwing flour tortillas? Since the revival of the show, Cornyation queens and empresses had commonly thrown objects at audience members—from foam footballs to wrapped condoms to candy. In the 1991 show, the final queen on stage was the Empress of Fiesta 100 of the Court of Outrageous Pretentiousness, celebrating the Fiesta centennial. The empress, her costume designed by Curt Slangal, came out in a taco-shaped dress that unfolded to reveal taco fixings. The empress threw tortillas at the audience, and they hurled them back at her with drunken enthusiasm. Thus a new tradition was born.

M: A HUSH FALLS OVER THE COURT

B: THE KING IS ALL A-TWITTER

M: AS WE AWAIT THE GRANDEST OF THE GRAND

B: WHO OUT-PRETENSES THE MOST OUTRAGEOUS PRETENSION OF ALL

M: THE EMPRESS OF OUR COURT

B: SHE'S THE MOB SCENE AT NIOSA

M: SHE'S THE MAD SCENE AT LA SEMANA

B: SHE'S THE RAGGEDY PEOPLE PARADE

M: SHE'S THE SOGGY RIVER PARADE

B: SHE'S THE BATTLE OF FLOWERS

M: SHE'S THE BATTLE OF FLOWERS WITH LIGHTS

B: SHE'S THE ORDURE OF THE ALAMO

M: SHE'S THE CANNY CAVALIERS

B: SHE'S FIZZELING FIREWORKS AND LACKLUSTER LASERS

M: SHE'S TOO MUCH TO EAT AND TOO LITTLE SLEEP

B: SHE'S AN EXHAUSTING ONSLAUGHT OF REVELRY

M: SHE'S PARTY-PARTY-PARTY

B: SHE'S THE GRANDEST

M: SHE'S THE GAUDIEST

B: THE GLITTERY-EST

M: THE GOSH AWFULLEST

B: REPRESENTING THE FIESTA CENTENNIAL

M: OUR EMPRESS OF THE COURT OF OUTRAGEOUS PRETENTIOUSNESS

_____*Ana*_____ OF THE HOUSE OF _*Banana*_

B: ATTENDED BY: _____

ROYAL ROBE DESIGNED BY: _____

Script excerpt, 1991.

In addition, Cornyation could now count on an active set of Cornyation fans who eagerly awaited the show every year and considered their participation crucial to its energy. According to longtime designer and stage manager Pat Wells, "It was a show before the curtains even opened." "They were high and they were buzzing, and the minute the curtains opened they would go, you couldn't stand it," Wells said. "There was a better show out there than there was on stage."[11] The show also began to attract a solid base of fans across the city, growing large enough to accommodate six shows in three nights during midweek of Fiesta week.

What appealed so much about the show to its longtime devoted fans in the 1990s? Most fans stressed the pleasure of dressing up, meeting people, and watching the show.[12] Many saw Cornyation as an opportunity to let go, relax, and just enjoy themselves without fear of judgment from others. As one person proclaimed, "Cornyation is about fun; it's about not taking yourselves too seriously. . . . You just have to enjoy it." Furthermore, many fans commented that the appeal of the show was the combination of the diverse crowd coming together to support a good cause in an entertaining fashion. According to one fan, "It doesn't matter what your culture, background, or color, or preference is—you know everybody's welcome at Cornyation and you really see all kinds of people." This growing fan base was also partly fueled by the dramatic growth (literally) of Cornyation costumes.

BIGGER AND BOLDER

Covering the show in a 1992 article in the *San Antonio Light*, journalist Robert Wynne described Cornyation as "Fiesta's funkiest royal-romping activities."[13] The event helped you "imagine what the 'real' queens, kings, and duchesses would look like if they came from an alternate Bizarro Superman world," he wrote.[14] With an impressively large stage and runway at Beethoven Hall, the show became more of a staged production. Increasing funding by sponsors allowed costumes to become grander in size and fashion. At the height of the bigger-and-bolder trend, in 1996, designers Larry Broom and Danny Geisler brought their duchess,

Terry Behal as the Duchess of Herman's Happiness, designed by Wayne Beers, Michael Bobo, Terry Behal, and Tim Yocorn. Court of Relentless Festivales, 1996. ▶

city councilwoman Lynda Billa Burke, onstage in a cherry picker, lifting her high above the audience. Decked out in a black leather bustier and pants, she was the Duchess of La Semana Alegre, representing gun permits.[15]

National events and issues in the 1990s such as Michael Jackson's pedophilia scandal, medical marijuana, sheep cloning, the dance song "Macarena," the arrest of O. J. Simpson, the impact of a California earthquake on the porn industry, and Tonya Harding's skating controversy were all fodder for Cornyation mockery as the show gave increasing attention to pop culture. In 1997 the show spoofed Madonna, Pat Boone, Princess Di, Dennis Rodman, and Barbie all in one night. Later Ray Chavez and Robert Rehm teamed up to represent Lorena Bobbitt and her surgical specialty.

Some of the show's most scathing commentary, however, was about local events. Cornyation mocked events of civic importance like San Antonio's recycling program, traffic gridlock, the Alamodome, and the battle between the Daughters of the Republic of Texas and Texas Parks and Wildlife for control of the Alamo.[16] In 1996 a duchess with manufactured proportions that would rival Dolly Parton's satirized controversy over the proposal for a topless bar on the River Walk. Pat Wells recalled that she felt like she became an established Cornyation designer the year she represented the demise of the *San Antonio Light* with a facsimile of the neon "Light" sign backed by Death catching up on the news. Wells had several of her friends read *Light* headlines in a recording studio to create eerie background music for her Empress of the Court.[17]

In 1993 Cornyation scriptwriters and designers mocked the dispute over who was the Rey Feo in Fiesta San Antonio, as for one year there were two kings due to internal disputes in LULAC. The emcees remarked: "You mean we now have a Rey Feo Uno and a Rey Feo Dos / Or a Tres or a Quatro or a—who knows where it will stop / You mean there is infighting in the minority group that represents the majority of our population / There are so many contenders that they may just have to have a Rey Feo parade to get them all in."[18] The Rey Feo figure was supported by LULAC and was considered to be the king for the city's Hispanic community, but the role of portraying him went to whichever man raised the

George Ann Simpson as the Empress of the Court of the Blazing Sun, designed by Pat Wells, 1993.   **105**

most money for LULAC scholarships.[19] Future King Anchovy Rick Casey wrote a column in the *San Antonio Express-News* that year proclaiming that Rey Feo was not the "people's king" but rather a "King Antonio Wannabe," desirous of the same prestige and hoopla during Fiesta. King Anchovy, Casey argued, was the real "people's king" or "ugly king."[20] For his part, King Anchovy continued to provide material for laughs—and to push the boundaries. When food critic Ron Bechtol became King Anchovy, he wrote a special column in the *San Antonio Light* titled "Anchovy Acceptance Comes from Years of Experimenting," making an allusion to sexual experimentation.[21]

The 1990s "culture wars" about lesbian and gay rights, artistry, marriage, and service in the military provided fodder for many innovative skits.[22] These political fights were coupled with dramatically increased representation of gay and lesbian experiences in the media, including the controversial airing in 1997 of a coming-out episode of the *Ellen* sitcom.[23] Bill Clinton's promise to issue an executive order removing the ban on lesbian and gay service in the military received the lion's share of public attention; the proposal was so controversial that it resulted instead in the military policy of "Don't Ask, Don't Tell," which allowed only closeted lesbian, gay, and bisexual service members.[24] In 1993 designer Larry Broom created a costume for the Queen of Mighty Mars, Representing Gays in the Military, that included "hand-grenade earrings and a bazooka scepter" along with a "camouflage-tent ball gown that hid some interesting surprises."[25] The emcees' commentary for this duchess ridiculed the tenor of the national debate over gays in the military:

> *Presenting the Queen of Mighty Mars*
> *Who storms onto the scene with a controversy most mighty*
> *Using her military might to rile the mighty military itself*
> *Raising questions of import—such as*
> *Will we need fuchsia foxholes?*
> *Will "Drop-the-soap" become the shower game of choice?*
> *Will "Dress-parade" take on a whole new meaning?*
> *Will "Fatigues by Calvin Klein" be the order of the day?*
> *Will the "Buddy system" gain a new significance?*
> *Will they need four sets of barracks instead of two?*

King Anchovy Rick Casey. Court of Relentless Festivales, 1996.

Will "Camp David" take on a whole new meaning?
Will "Flamethrower" become the weapon of choice?
Will "Throw another faggot on the fire" actually refer to firewood?
Will licentious, lascivious lechery really become the "order of the day"?
Will the men and women who serve our country finally receive the honor
and respect that they deserve?[26]

This satire criticized the direction of the national debate about gays in the military, which focused disproportionately on gay men and the potential discomfort they could cause heterosexual military men sharing close quarters, such as locker rooms, with them. Scriptwriter Bob Jolly ridiculed the assumption that the open presence of gay men would feminize the military through jokes about fuchsia foxholes and cross-dressing during "dress parades."

There were some limits to Cornyation's humor and critiques. The 1993 Cornyation script initially included recurring jokes about the "Brunch Davidians" and the "Queen of Kinky Sects," a joke about the ongoing standoff between the Branch Davidian religious sect and federal and Texas law enforcement in Waco. But when the Federal Bureau of Investigation launched an assault on April 19, 1993, that led to the death of more than seventy adults and children, organizers pulled the skit and its jokes the week before Cornyation. According to the designer, "It felt too soon." The skit was run the next year instead.

One of the show's biggest changes in the 1990s was that it began to incorporate drag and larger production numbers. Most of the Bonham Exchange performances involved just a duchess performing, typically with a limited entourage. This entourage grew at the Beethoven Hall as the duchess or queen was increasingly surrounded by other performers, including men in drag. In 1992 Latino designer John McBurney joined Cornyation, contributing to the show's aesthetic drag and a playful artistic style that used repeating themes in costumes. McBurney's first numbers included a spoof of the Mary Kay cosmetics convention and a mockery of the Bill Clinton and Monica Lewinsky affair, with a central figure of Bill Clinton surrounded by men and women in blue dresses. McBurney and his partner, Michael Marmontello, became known as "the multiples." Starting in 1994 the entertainment for King Anchovy included the Pointless Sisters, a drag number pulled together for the show by mainly Latino men. Their colorful performances at times included traditional Mexican ballet folklórico along with more typical drag acts.

FLIRTING WITH RESPECTABILITY

In Cornyation's first year at Beethoven Hall, a newspaper reporter quipped that the show was "flirting with respectability," moving closer into the mainstream. At the time, LGBT visibility in the United States was undergoing record growth. From the public coming out of Ellen DeGeneres on her television show to the

◄ *Top: Raquel Riojas as the Empress of the Würstfest and attendants, designed by John McBurney. Court of Relentless Festivals, 1996. **Middle:** Kristin Nelson as the Empress of the Impeachment Ordeal with attendants, designed by John McBurney. Court of Everyday Soap Operas, 1999. **Bottom:** The Pointless Sisters. Court of the Blazing Sun, 1993.*

culture wars against gay rights, LGBT culture was not only more visible than it had ever been in the past, but also often pushing closer to gaining mainstream respectability. Lesbian rights leader Urvashi Vaid argues that lesbians and gay men in the 1990s were only achieving "virtual equality," though, not true equality, because of this pressure to mainstream.[27]

Cornyation began to get a lot of attention from the broader community. It became a regular part of the King Antonio and Rey Feo Fiesta schedule; King Anchovy was also recognized now as official "unofficial royalty" by the Fiesta Commission. When the show satirized the controversy over the (very purple) color of renowned author Sandra Cisneros's house, Cisneros herself attended the performance.[28] When Pat Wells was designing an uncomplimentary skit about the political battle between Lila Cockrell and Nelson Wolff, the Cockrell campaign office called her and asked her to change the skit, which Wells refused to do.[29] In 1995 Robert Rehm designed the Queen of the Enchilada Roja in honor of the new downtown library designed by Ricardo Legorreta and painted "enchilada red." Duchess Susan Yerkes recalled, "I appeared as a giant 'Bookworm,' and Robert's costume was so wonderful that the city invited Robert to bring the Bookworm back later that spring to ride in a downtown parade for the library grand opening. I rode on a flatbed trailer in the parade just behind then-governor George W. Bush, his wife Laura, and Legorreta. I believe that may be the only time a Cornyation character has had equal parade billing with a soon-to-be U.S. president (and a Republican, at that)."[30]

As Cornyation became more visible and established in the 1990s, "unofficial" Fiesta events, including house parties and smaller parades, proliferated. Two gay men, Don and Harry, on the outskirts of town bought and renovated a group of nearby homes, called the Compound. They threw an annual Fiesta parade and party there. This informal event was attended by LGBT individuals and also city elites; one attendee remembers running into the mayor, Lila Cockrell. Cornyation extended beyond the show to after-parties and events at the Bonham, along with private events like the Battle of the Flour Tortillas Parade, which was held

Top: King Anchovy David Risher with Rey Feo. Court of Outrageous Pretentiousness, 1991. *Middle:* George Ann Simpson as Queen of the Mayor's Race, designed by Pat Wells. Court of Outrageous Pretentiousness, 1991. *Bottom:* Susan Yerkes, Queen of the Enchilada Roja, designed by Robert Rehm. Court of Glorious Grease, 1995. ▶

at Braune's house in the early 1990s. Cast members would bring their costumes to "show the costumes one last time before they were tossed in the garbage or fell apart," Braune remembered. "So it just sort of evolved into a parade because it was a way to show the costumes."[31]

The LGBT community regularly appeared in the King William Parade and made some inroads into other official events. In 1997 a brief column in the gay and lesbian newspaper the *Marquise* proclaimed that "gay and lesbian history was made once again in San Antonio" when a "funky, 'family' float flouts Fiesta Flambeau."[32] The Gay and Lesbian Community Center identified itself as the "Red Ribbon Food Program" and launched a float with strobe lights and "blaring disco performances of Donna Summer, the Village People and Sylvester accompanied by outrageously attired, lip-syncing queens."[33]

There also was a proliferation of Cornyation . . . stuff. In the late 1980s the directors began making Fiesta medals for sale to the general public. In the 1990s each designer began to make medals, many handmade, for his or her individual skit. Before long there was Cornyation artwork and Cornyation T-shirts. The first Cornyation poster was designed by Danny Geisler. A promotional video with actor Jesse Borrego, directed by Michael Mehl, included many Cornyation cast members.

ANSWERING THE HIV/AIDS CRISIS

For its first twenty-five years, Cornyation devoted itself to fundraising for SALT. In 1991, as the HIV/AIDS epidemic accelerated and Cornyation's directors became disgruntled with the lack of SALT involvement, the event was transformed into a nonprofit foundation dedicated to fundraising for charities, with an emphasis on HIV/AIDS and other health services. In 1992 the Cornyation program announced that it was a fundraiser for Arts for Life, a nonprofit foundation of artists who promoted HIV/AIDS awareness and raised money for the proliferating and financially struggling HIV/AIDS service organizations in the city.[34] Throughout the 1990s the show benefited several HIV/AIDS service organizations, including Blue Light Candle, Providence Home, San Antonio AIDS Foundation, and Alamo

Cari Hill, Vice-Empress of the Court of Outrageous Pretentiousness, designed by Brad Braune and Tom McKenzie, 1991.

Cover of Cornyation Video Shoot in the Marquise, *April 1996.*

Area Resource Center. The show also benefited organizations like Project Heart, a program geared toward placing counselors in high-risk middle schools. The amount of money raised each year was small at first; in 1993 the show netted only $3,000 for charity. But after the 1999 show the Cornyation Foundation, Inc., dished out $30,000 to charities and could boast having raised a grand total of about $110,000 in the 1990s.[35]

During the 1980s and most of the 1990s, HIV/AIDS service organizations grew, struggled, and perished. Many of the earliest service organization efforts arose out of the flourishing gay and lesbian bar life in San Antonio. The Bar Tavern Guild began in the 1980s as a coordinated response to AIDS by the gay bar owners in the city. One of these owners, Robert Edwards, also known as Papa Bear, played a critical part in the Tavern Guild and later in the formation of the San Antonio AIDS Foundation (SAAF). SAAF was founded in 1986 as an all-volunteer hospice in the back of the bar and was one of the first sustained efforts at HIV/AIDS community-based organization in Bexar County.[36]

Cornyation itself was being transformed by the impact of the epidemic. Throughout the 1990s each program memorialized multiple men involved in the show who had passed away in the previous year. Former King Anchovy and Cornyation designer Tom McKenzie recalled, "We lost so many people in that time period. Every year it was like two or three, or maybe five people. It was just horrible. We had all these extremely talented people . . . just GONE, right at the height of their career. . . . This organization was probably hit more than any other, except for theater or musical companies. . . . Those were sad times." [37]

The reconfiguration of Cornyation as an HIV/AIDS fundraiser attracted a new set of designers who were committed to fundraising. Small business owners like Bill Davis, Danny Spears, Wayne Beers, Michael Bobo, and Oscar Morales stepped up to design for Cornyation. Davis remarked that part of his motivation was knowing that "the outcome was going to be beneficial to health."[38]

Fundraising for AIDS service organizations was not just a part of Cornyation but a new Fiesta event. In the 1990s a group of professional gay men created a new fundraiser: the WEBB Party. This event began as a backyard barbecue fundraiser, an idea originator Bill Hudson got from the Austin Octopus Party, which raised money for AIDS Services of Austin. The original name, the Web Party, referred to an Ethiopian proverb about many spiders tying up a lion in their web. When Hudson forgot to spellcheck the invitation, the spelling of the WEBB Party stuck.[39] Initially a fundraising party for the San Antonio AIDS Foundation held by friends and acquaintances, the party eventually became an official Fiesta event. SAAF took over the lucrative event in 2000 when the party "was on its last leg" due to the exhaustion of its organizers.[40]

Cornyation in the 1990s was bigger and bolder, both in the size of its costumes and in the show's scale. The newfound corporate sponsorship of individual duchesses led to some of the most grandiose costuming in Cornyation history. The event's move to Beethoven Hall suggested that it was dabbling with respectability, although the show was still as bawdy and critical as it had been in its earlier years. One of the show's biggest changes was its transformation from a fundraiser for SALT to one dedicated to nonprofit organizations across the city, with an emphasis on HIV/AIDS service organizations.

■ ■ ■

Lite *The Official Beer of Fiesta* PRESENTS

CORNYATION XXXIII - '98

The Court of Comic Book Characters

A Benefit For : Project Heart, San Antonio AIDS Foundation, & The Providence Home

Entertainment For The House
Lina del Roble

The Order of the A-Corn
Arrival of King Anchovy XXXIII
The Ruler and Sovereign Head of Cornyation 1998 The Court of Comic Book Characters : Rick Hunter
Designers: Leon Bridges & Jose Luis Uresti • *Attended by*: Elisa Partida
(dress by Mr. Jim) & Shelbi Jary (dress by Adriene Rojas)

Entertainment For The King
"Caribbean Shakedown" / Culture In Motion Dance Group

THE COURT

Representing the The Flintstones
The Duchess of the Quarry Market : Nyla of the House of Alcala
Designer: Kim Marks, Wayne Beers, Wendy Smith & Michael Bobo • *Attended by*: Rod Gonzales,
Stephen Warner, & Lee Spruiell • *Sponsored by*: W.D. Deli and The Marks Design Group

Representing Marmaduke
The Duchess of Mama - Duke : Oscar of the House of Camacho
Designer: Janel Hradil • *Attended by*: William Pullin, Janel Hradil, & Kathy Sharp • *Music by*: John Grosskopf
Sponsored by: On Main Card Shop

Representing the Dilbert Zone
The Duchess of Hale-Bopp Comet & Heaven's Gate : Connie of the House of Brenner
Designers: Jerry Wilkerson, Wendy Carter, & Connie Brenner • *Attended by*: Felipe Garrido, John, Laura, Hootie, Erwin,
Lisa, Bruce and a cast of thousands • *Sponsored by*: aArtvarks and J W Tulips Floral & Events Design

Entertainment For The Court
South Coast Invasion

Representing Rocky the Flying Squirrel
The Queen of John Glenn's Space Effect : George Ann of the House of Simpson
Designers: Pat Wells & Penny Davis • *Attended by*: Patti David, Darrell Fritter, Jose Cruz, & Amy La Presto
Sponsored by: Jim Geist & Edward Alanis - (Most Eminent Real Estate Professionals of the Court of High Stakes, Guy Chipman, Co. Realtors)

Representing Josie & The Pussy Cats
The Queen of The Spice Girls : Connie Lee of the House of Walker
Designers: Danny Spear, Oscar Morales & Fernando Arias • *Attended by*: Cyndi Avila, Sondra Klamm, Cecil Starke,
Cynthia Clark & The designers • *Sponsored by*: Land of Was Antiques

Representing Cow & Chicken
The Queen Oprah & the Mad Cow Disease : Marye of the House of Saunders
Designers: Tom McKenzie, Bill Gage, & Ric Minks • *Music by*: Donnie Neubauer & Keith Harter
Thanks to: Ann Egerton & Balloon Expressions

Representing Wonder Woman
The Queen of The School District Scandal : Lisa of the House of Suarez
Designer: John McBurney • *Attended by*: John McBurney, Mike Marmontello, Sergio Moreno,
Rex Anderson, Felipe, Lozano, Marcus Cerda, & Art Ramos • *Sponsored by*: Kim Bunch

Entertainment For The Court
The Pointless Sisters

Representing Little Orphan Annie
The Vice Empress of The Presidential Deep Throat Divas : Maria of the House of Moore
Designers: Terry Behal, John "JP" Pollard & Tim Yocom
Attended by: Jeff Strong • *Sponsored by*: Bonham Exchange

Representing Ripley's Believe It or Not
The Empress of Purple Paint : Dawnita of the House of Brooks
Designer: Daniel Geisler
Attended by: Jeff "Buck" Strong, The voice of Bonnie Victor Fried, Mariachis and Special Guests from the Court of Public Opinion:
Susan Yerkes, Rick Casey, Mike Greenberg and Mike Casey. • *Special Thanks to*: Debra Guerrero, Karine Berghauser, Bart Nichols,
Allie and Greg Vallery, Ann and Bob Geisler, Gloria Arecchi and Lewis Fisher • *Sponsored by*: An Anonymous Friend

---

Program Notes

Show Director: .... Greg Moczygemba	Logo Development: .... Robert "Beto" Gonzalez,
Show Coordinator: .... Ray Chavez	.... Bob Underwood, & Ray Chavez
Narrators: .... Brenda Ray & Ken Slavin	Preshow Music: .... "The Inimitable" Robert Garcia
Brenda Ray's Costume provided by:	Secretary / Treasurer: .... John Peck
.... Graciela Creations in the Yard	Crew: .... Mark Porter, Tovas Brown,
Entertainment Coordinator: .... Dawn Moczygemba	.... Eric Slade & Billy Stinnett
Box Office: ...... Mike Hons, Sally Dunaisky & Joseph Trevino	Volunteer Coordinator .... Bob Weeks
Cornyation Theme Composed & Recorded by: .... Michael Mehl	Advertising and Program: .... Brad Shaw
Overture by: .... Spike Jones	
Sound Person: .... Gabe Garza	*Dedicated to the Memory of*
Poster Design: .... Robert "Beto" Gonzalez	*Daryl Engel • Shelton DuBoise • Steve Collier*

Program, 1998.

MORE QUEENS THAN YOU EXPECTED

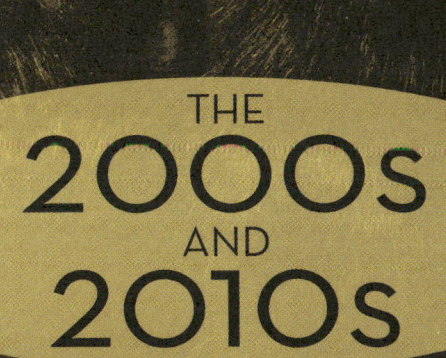

The stage lights go up on four huge billboard-size set pieces painted red and lettered in white with the slogan "I'm a Mormon." A man depicting 2012 Republican presidential candidate Mitt Romney wears a suit with a tail of money streaming behind him. Other Republican candidates prance in front of the set pieces in a parade. A fluffy white feather boa streams behind the performer representing candidate Rick Santorum, in homage to the revengeful and intentional sexual neologism invented by gay columnist Dan Savage to share the politician's name. As they exit, a man dressed as a detective sneaks across the stage to the theme song of the *Pink Panther* and covers up the second "M" in the sign, leaving the slogan "I'm a Moron." The skit quickly devolves into a treatment of Mayan predictions of the end of the world. The set pieces come apart and open up to show Mayan iconography on their reverse sides. A fly descends and announces "Welcome to the Apocalypse." The Republican candidates strip down to boxers and T-shirts and dance around with signs about impending apocalypse. The "Empress of Mormons, Morons & Mayans (oh my)" moves to center stage in a flowing patriotic gown and sparkling headpiece. As she marches around the stage, her gown reveals a skimpy Mayan costume, and she eventually eats the plastic red heart from a sacrificed Barack Obama. After her finale, the empress's designer, Chris Sauter, and his cast stride across the stage as the emcee announces them. More than one hundred cast members have been waiting anxiously in the wings to make their curtain call. As stage manager Pat Wells yells the name of each empress, her cast marches across the stage and out the back door of the theater to the throng of fans waiting for them.[1]

Attendant to the Empress of Mormons, Morons & Mayans (oh my), designed by Chris Sauter. Court of Never Ending Endings, 2012.

Josie Molina as the Empress of Mormons, Morons & Mayans (oh my) and attendants, designed by Chris Sauter. Court of Never Ending Endings, 2012.

When Cornyation moved into the Charline McCombs Empire Theatre in 2000 it underwent several dramatic changes. With a large audience and no runway, designers couldn't rely on the subtlety of the duchesses' costuming to communicate their message. Instead, the production developed into a sketch comedy show with a yearly cast of more than one hundred. New designers and performers entered the show, as some designers aged, died, or moved on to other artistic ventures. With the bigger venue and six shows during each Fiesta, Cornyation became a major Fiesta fundraiser in the 2000s and 2010s, donating more than one million dollars to local charities, most of which were HIV/AIDS service organizations.

YOUR FOUR MINUTES OF FAME

On the Empire stage, before a small bedroom window, two men dressed in pajamas and slippers portray brothers John and Michael Darling from *Peter Pan*. A tall, leggy drag queen in a puffy green dress and wings joins them onstage. When Michael, clutching his teddy bear, asks, "Are you a fairy?" the queen proclaims, "Oh, honey, I'm a BIG fairy!" She promises to take them to a real play party "that's on the second pop star to the right and on till morning" as they go off to Neverland. They dance to the song "Ease on Down the Road" from *The Wiz* as the set opens to reveal a Michael Jackson impersonator and a larger set with a canopy bed. The word "Neverland" glitters on the canopy. Several muscular "Lost Boys" come out in pajama pants and white T-shirts, carrying pillows, as the music changes to the song "ABC" by the Jackson 5. The music lingers on the lyrics from the song about learning about love as the Jackson character encourages the Lost Boys to provocatively peel off their T-shirts. As the Jackson impersonator seductively touches the Lost Boys, the music suddenly shifts to Jackson's later hit "Black or White" as four tall men dressed as pirates march onstage and begin to dance in a kick line with Jackson. Finally, Carolyn Davalos, the Empress of the Neverland Pajama Party, enters the stage to music from "The Way You Make Me Feel." Dressed as a stylish Captain Hook with a trailing coat and short shorts, Davalos confronts Jackson as the music shifts to "Beat It." The pirates and Lost Boys begin to dance antagonistically against each other, as Jackson and the Lost Boys engage in provocative dance moves. Finally, the fairy Tinkerbell from the start of the show comes between the two sets of dancers and, as the music stops, proclaims, "I'm a BIG FAIRY." Then, behind her, the whole cast begins to dance to music from "Thriller." The skit about the purported pedophilic predilections of Michael Jackson ends the 2004 Court of Chaotic Clashing Cultures.[2]

Cornyation was transformed by its new home in the Empire Theatre in downtown San Antonio. The Empire shares a backstage with the Majestic Theatre, which in the 2000s was the largest theater venue in town. The wider stage and lack of a runway necessitated the show's shift from the spectacle of a duchess or empress parading down a runway to a sketch comedy show. Designer and stage manager Pat Wells described the new version as "musical *Beach Blanket Babylon.*" "If you haven't seen that," Wells added, "I'd describe it as the campiest version of a coronation you've ever seen."[3] In its transformation into a sketch comedy show, the production grew larger, as more cast members were included in each skit, and the role of the duchess and her costume became less significant. Instead of locating the critique of politics and culture on the duchess's outfit and in the introduction to the skit, each designer filled his or her four minutes onstage with a combination of music, dancing, spoken words, sight gags, reversals of plot, and interactions between characters to tell a short story about a social or political issue. At least one element of the original show, however, remained the same—each skit features a woman playing a queen or empress.[4]

The focus of the show—its critique of local and national politics through corny, campy satire, and its mocking of Fiesta traditions—also remained mostly the

Clockwise from top: The Pointless Sisters, Court of New Beginnings, 2013; Member of the Pointless Sisters, Court of Never Ending Endings, 2012; Theresa Machado as the Duchess of Miss Grande USA, designed by John McBurney, Court of Playfully Petulant Periodicals, 2003.

same. And when it came to local concerns to parody, the twenty-first century provided plenty of fodder. When national attention was drawn in 2011 to the dethroning of Miss Fiesta, seventeen-year-old Domonique Ramirez, whom one of the Miss Fiesta organizers reportedly told to lose weight and "get off the tacos," Cornyation designers responded with a satire of the beauty queen's predicament (the Queen of the Taco-Tarnished Tiara).[5] At Cornyation, local drag act the Pointless Sisters have mocked San Antonio's Fiesta recycling program, its mayor's Get Fit exercise campaign, and plans for a new downtown streetcar. Critiques were occasionally more pointed, criticizing gentrification, nepotism, anti-gay politicians, and a cockroach infestation in public housing projects. In 2003, after controversy over the Miss USA pageant coming to San Antonio, designer John McBurney parodied the candidates. "Several men dressed as beauty queens shimmy across the stage," the *Express-News* reported. "Pennsylvania is dressed up as cream cheese. Virginia wears a silver tray and ham on her head, while Kentucky balances a big bucket of chicken on her head."[6]

Ballet San Antonio and choreographer Gabriel Zertuche. Court of New Beginnings, 2013.

The show was still attentive to national political scandals and trends, as well—particularly presidential politics. A *Wizard of Oz*–themed sketch in 2000 mocked presidential candidates: George Bush was depicted as the Scarecrow, "with a tiny little brain (and precariously dangling corncob)"; Al Gore was an "ax-stroking Tin Man."[7] The skit employed much lesbian romanticism: Dorothy had the hots for Glenda, the Good Witch of the North, and lesbian icons Xena and sidekick Gabrielle made appearances as wedding witnesses.[8] In later years, Sarah Palin became a rich topic of satire; designers created multiple skits about her Alaskan heritage, outlandish sayings, and pregnant daughter. Designer Andy Sanchez criticized Arizona's new anti-immigrant law with his 2011 Queen of Arizona à la Mode, portraying the Arizona governor as cartoon hunter Elmer Fudd and Latino immigrants as hardworking contributors to the economy. Democratic and progressive politics did not escape lampooning either: in 2008 the show mocked Barack Obama's initial struggles wooing black voters.

In the twenty-first century, the content of the show broadened to include foibles of celebrities and the country's obsession with reality television.[9] One year designers named a skit "The Amazing Race for Who Wants to Be America's Next Top Presidential Idol," mocking multiple reality television shows at once. In 2008 designer Leora Uribe created a skit about Angelina Jolie's baby boom, which ended in a grand finale featuring the Queen of Brad Pitt's Nightmare;

Drawing of same-sex marriage skit costuming, Robert Rehm, 2004.

the queen's oversized pregnant belly birthed twenty dolls and stuffed animals tied to a long rope. The comic gag was watching the dolls as they were drawn out of the queen's womb. As the *Express-News* reported, "The over-the-top skit became more ridiculous as backup dancers draped the rope with dangling dolls over shoulders for a group dance routine."[10] Other skits mocked the infidelities of golf star Tiger Woods and the diabetes of cook and show host Paula Dean.

The show also still fearlessly tackles LGBT issues. Skits about same-sex marriage, Don't Ask, Don't Tell, and gay Boy Scouts became regular fare. When Mayor Julian Castro was grand marshal of the city's 2009 Pride Parade, Cornyation designers parodied his support of the LGBT community. Hipsters' predilections for food trucks in front of the gay bars in town were the subject of one sketch in 2012.

Long before same-sex marriage was legal in Texas, John McBurney organized a skit with innovative costuming, in which cast members wore suits that transformed into wedding gowns in the middle of the performance.[11] In 2013 the Ballet San Antonio entertainment for the king included an homage to same-sex marriage. Initially male and female dancers danced in conventional pairings, but halfway through the song, male-male and female-female couplings took over the performance. Ballet San Antonio director Gabriel Zertuche walked onstage holding a sign with a red square with pink equal sign, the symbol for marriage equality.

Leora Uribe as Queen of Give Peas a Chance, designed by Dom Gonzalez and Leora Uribe. Court of New Beginnings, 2013.

The use of camp, reversals, and big reveals are still a central part of the show. Performers frequently transform costumes and set pieces on stage in the middle of their four-minute performances. A 1950s kitchen becomes a dominatrix dungeon to parody the popular novel *Fifty Shades of Grey*. Designers mash up unexpected themes. In a critique of the prohibition of women drivers in Saudi Arabia, women on stage shed their burkas to reveal characters from the show *Sex in the City*. A skit about the National Rifle Association and gun control turns into one about zombies dancing to Michael Jackson's iconic "Thriller" when the emcees unexpectedly shoot at the ensemble. The duchess is often revealed midway through the skit during a pivotal plot point; in a critique of childhood obesity in San Antonio, designer and duchess Leora Uribe arrives dressed as a slice of pizza to taunt the children.

THERE IS NO DRESS REHEARSAL

There are some ways that the show has changed in recent decades. According to designer Robert Rehm, the show has "lost that sort of naïve, kitschy, found-art

Ricardo Muñoz dancing as Pointless Sister. Court of Festive Fetes and Frivolous Faux Pas, 2014.

sort of throw-together-what-you-can-find" feel.[12] According to another designer, now it has become "six months of fund-raising with some groups, and they've got T-shirts and they've got professionally made [Fiesta] medals and they've got carpenters and all this sort of stuff, so they've sort of upped their game, if you will." "It's become a much more professional, deliberate production than it has [been] in the past," the designer concluded. In 2002, newcomer Rene Roberts, a Latino hairdresser and drag artist, effectively raised funds to create spectacular

Designer Rene Roberts and Michael Marmontello backstage. Court of Chaotic Clashing Cultures, 2004.

costuming and set pieces. He quickly became known for the intricacy of his costumes. Although individual designers seek corporate sponsorship for their costumes, makeup, and set pieces, the show itself has never actively sought corporate sponsorship.

With so many cast members, many of whom are unknown to the organizers and were brought in as friends of the participants, Ray Chavez and the Cornyation Board of Directors had to create more regulations about show content and cast member behavior backstage. Although the show still promoted itself as the "raunchiest and cheapest event" in Fiesta, it also, over time, formally disallowed full nudity, lewd behavior such as simulated sex, and extreme violence. One Cornyation board member explained that "it's not because we're trying to be, you know, a family show or anything like that." Rather, the board became concerned about remaining an official Fiesta event and maintaining good relations with the Empire Theatre. Other issues also impeded some of the fun. When a woman in the audience was struck in the head with something hard during the 2005 show, the resulting lawsuit caused a ban on most flying objects, including the beloved tortillas. The plaintiff settled for a cash settlement of less than $1,000 and ten tickets to the 2006 show.[13]

The new larger scale of the show has not altered the emphasis on fun, spontaneity, and amateurism that has remained from the earliest shows in the 1950s. There is still no dress rehearsal for the show, leaving the first show of Tuesday night predictably chaotic. According to designer Jesse Mata, "It's a little bit of a train wreck." "The audience is always wondering, 'Oh my God, whose costume is going to fall apart?'" Mata explained. "Or, you know, 'What drag queen's going to fall off the stage or whatever?' And we've had crazy things happen, you know?"[14] Older fans and designers are opinionated and divided about the new, bigger spectacle of Cornyation. Many of them are proud that Cornyation has grown into a community institution with such diversity of performers. But these fans and designers also contend that the show has changed too dramatically. Some older fans and designers claim that the show has become more focused on the theatrics rather than the visual design of the duchesses' dresses. "Sometimes you can't even tell which woman is the queen," one designer told me. Cornyation board paperwork the designers filled out in the 2000s (and still do today) began

More Queens Than You Expected

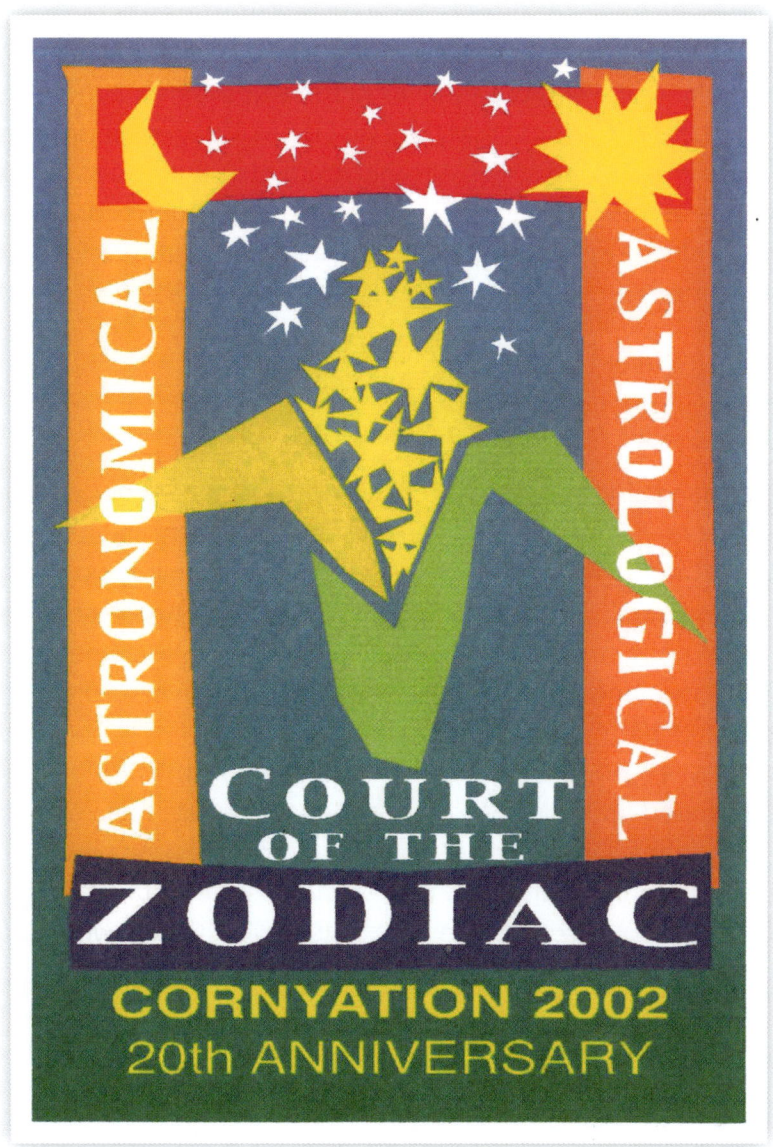

Show imagery, 2002.

with a reminder: "We will focus our production on the queens, their gowns, and the designers' creativity. REMEMBER: The audience must be able to easily identify your queen. Our queens are always female."[15] A few former designers have voiced nostalgia for when the show used to be "more gay." Longtime directors Chavez and Jolly are insistent that the event is not a "gay event," in that the show is open and welcoming to all San Antonio residents.[16] But some fans and designers reminisce about the days when the show was performed at the Bonham Exchange, and express concern about the increasing number of heterosexual men and women who serve as designers for Cornyation.

STILL THE HOTTEST TICKET IN TOWN

One huge change in Fiesta that can largely be traced back to Cornyation is the dramatic increase in LGBT-friendly events and attendance at these events by diverse San Antonio residents. I thought about this proliferation and diversity in 2014 when I attended the "hat party," an informal Fiesta event. The party was held just down the street from my house, and a friend who had just moved to the city and I went together. Neither of us had ever been to the hat party before. The purpose of the event is to wear huge, elaborate Fiesta hats and to drink mimosas for a few hours in a private backyard before the Battle of the Flowers parade. My friend and I both sported store-bought hats that we covered with flowers and Lotería game cards affixed with rhinestones and glitter. On our way to the party, my friend remarked that everyone had told him that Fiesta had been "taken over by Mexicans and gays." And indeed the hat party is filled with Latino gay men in huge spectacular hats, but there are also other members of the LGBT community and an increasing number of heterosexuals who come out to enjoy one of the most relaxed and colorful parties in town.

The number of events one could attend in San Antonio as a researcher studying LGBT experiences in urban festivals is almost overwhelming. Official LGBT-friendly events like the Cornyation, the WEBB Party, and the Chili Queens Chili Cookoff at the Bonham Exchange flourish. As one of the longest-running LGBT-positive events, Cornyation gets more recognition now that it did in the past; when Ray Chavez reached his thirtieth year of directing the show in 2013, the Fiesta Commission recognized his achievement. Cornyation also recognized Chavez with a special thirtieth-anniversary medal commemorating his dedication to the show and organization. Cornyation fundraising dispersal is more regularly covered in the press than previously; and a recent exhibit at the Institute of Texan Cultures included a photograph of Cornyation in the history of the Fiesta. Many newspapers refer to the show as "perennially one of the hottest Fiesta tickets in town."[17]

Unofficial Fiesta events such as the Project Fiesta barbecue, the Fiesta Frenzy drag show, and the Fiesta Madness party raise funds for causes across the city. The Fiesta Frenzy frequently raises funds for explicitly LGBT-positive causes, including the San Antonio College LGBT group and a well-known drag queen called Shady Lady.[18] In addition to the importance and visibility of these fundraisers is the appropriation by and mass attendance of LGBT people at major Fiesta events. LGBT attendees could take the shuttle from the strip of bars near downtown to the unofficial "gay night" at NIOSA or watch the Battle of the Flowers parade in front of the Menger Hotel.

Of course, many LGBT people find Fiesta distasteful—too drunk, too loud, too hard to find parking, too racist. The same year I attended the hat party, a medal stating that "Fiesta Is Racist" was distributed by the Esperanza Peace and Justice Center, a long-standing organization run by Latina lesbians in a broader coalition of organizers working against social injustice in South Texas.[19] Even with this dissension, there is no doubt that the LGBT community is very visible during Fiesta San Antonio.

MORE QUEENS THAN YOU EXPECTED

In the 2000s Cornyation began successfully to woo high-profile Kings Anchovy from the realms of business, politics, and the arts. Rather than showing up at the first show, the king began to get involved in hosting pre-Fiesta events, touring as royalty during the festival to other events, and fundraising. The local media began to announce the king in advance of Cornyation and to include him or her in announcements of other Fiesta royalty. In 2002 King Anchovy James Lifshutz

King Anchovy Andrew Weissman. Court of Never Ending Endings, 2012.

Invitation for the First King Anchovy Ball, 2000.

was featured in a *San Antonio Express-News* profile of Fiesta royalty. Lifshutz admitted that he used to be a Texas Cavalier and was selected one year to be King Antonio, but "when I told them I couldn't afford it, they made me resign."[20] The next year King Anchovy XXXVIII, Bart Nichols, a local dentist, was featured in a color spread with King Antonio and El Rey Feo as the three kings of Fiesta. Cornyation royalty also became more diverse in the 2000s. The 2000 and 2001 shows were an auspicious start to the new decade at the Empire Theatre. The 2000 show began with the presentation of its King Anchovy, Centro Alameda

King Anchovy Debra Guerrero backstage with designer John McBurney. Court of Radically Raucous Unreal Radio, 2001.

chairman Henry Muñoz III, "who was carried onstage on a litter like Cleopatra by four scantily clad men, body-painted purple."[21] Muñoz had achieved the rank of Fiesta royalty already, as Rey Feo in 1998, but King Anchovy was a new accomplishment. Muñoz threw a huge ball at the end of his reign, the King Anchovy Ball of 2000.

In 2001 Cornyation fans were surprised to find an atypical King Anchovy, the then-councilwoman Debra Guerrero, who was close friends with Muñoz and had been part of multiple royalty entourages with him. As the first female King Anchovy, Guerrero went all out, performing not just in the king's opening number but as the Queen of the Political Olympics for designers John McBurney and Eddie Reyes. Guerrero was followed by two other female Kings Anchovy—journalist Elaine Wolff in 2007 and city manager Sheryl Sculley in 2009—and the first Queen Anchovy—Jody Bailey Newman, who co-reigned with her husband Steve Newman, King Anchovy XLIX. In 2016 the show for the first time had two kings, as the couple Michael Bobo and Wayne Beers reigned as the Kings Anchovy LI.

Newman wasn't the only unexpected queen. In 2012, due to a renovation of its regular venue, the Coronation relocated to the Majestic Theatre, which adjoins the Empire Theatre. On Wednesday night, both Coronation and Cornyation were performed. The area outside both stage doors, which are in close proximity, became a lively mix of tuxedoed fathers of debutantes taking smoke breaks and men costumed as Twinkies. There were concerns that Cornyation would disrupt the formal event next door, and the narrow door that divided the two backstage

The Political Olympics – Cornyation 2001

BOB   WELCOME BACK ONE AND ALL AS WE CONTINUE TO PRESENT TO YOU OUR QUEENS OF THE COURT

RAY   AND IF YOU THINK IT WAS CONFUSING TO HAVE A WOMAN FOR THE KING – YOU AIN'T READY FOR WHAT'S NEXT

BOB   FOR, WHILE YOU WERE OUT FRESHENING YOUR LIBATION

RAY   THERE JUST HAPPENS TO HAVE BEEN A VAST TRANSFORMATION

BOB   THIS REALLY MUST BE ONE FOR THE RECORD BOOKS

RAY   AND THINGS REALLY AREN'T ALWAYS THE WAY THEY FIRST LOOK

BOB   FOR THIS ONE – YOU DON'T GET A STORY

RAY   JUST A FEW CLUES

BOB   REMEMBER THE SCANDAL ABOUT THE CONVENTION CENTER GOING OVER BUDGET ?

RAY   AND A RIDDLE: WHO'S GOT WHAT WE WANT, WHO'S GOT WHAT WE NEED?

BOB   HINT: WHO'S GOT MUSCULAR LEGS, OVAL EYES AND A DEEP CHEST?

RAY   AND WHAT DOES THAT HINT HAVE TO DO WITH ANYTHING AT ALL?

BOB   I THINK THIS WHOLE SECTION HAS JUST GONE TO THE DOGS

RAY   SO WITHOUT FURTHER ADO WE PRESENT TO YOU

BOB   THE QUEEN OF THE POLITICAL OLYMPICS

RAY   REPRESENTING THE GUIDING LIGHT

BOB   DEBRA OF THE HOUSE OF GUERRERO

RAY   WHO AS YOU MAY RECALL WAS THE KING BEFORE YOU WENT AWAY TO GET ANOTHER DRINK!

BOB   AND THE DESIGNER OF THIS MADNESS: JOHN MCBURNEY

Co designer Eddie Reyes

Script excerpt, 2001.

King Anchovy Steve Newman and Queen Anchovy Jody Newman in the King William Parade, 2014.

Kings Anchovy Michael Bobo and Wayne Beers

Emcee Rick Frederick practicing his Coronation of the Queen bow in front of Fiesta Commission member and fellow emcee Elaine Wolff. Court of Never Ending Endings, 2012.

areas was guarded during showtime. One Cornyation organizer claimed that "they had everything but the army reserve out there with their M-16s" the first year. On the first evening, stage manager and longtime designer Pat Wells was checking the downstairs area and noticed some Cornyation props and costumes piled out in the hallway outside a dressing room. "Come to find out it was some mother of one of the [Coronation] duchesses who didn't want their dressing room because it was too small, so they moved [the Cornyation designer's stuff]." Wells found the mother in question and reminded her that Cornyation was the one sharing their space; she insisted the mother move her belongings back to the Majestic side of the backstage. When the mother protested, Wells warned her, "You don't understand at all, that this is going to happen, and you're going to do it with my help or you're going to do it listening to the queen whose stuff this belongs to."[22] Cornyation reacted to this change in its typical satirical style. The 2012 imagery for the show included the tagline "More Queens Than You Expected," and emcee Rick Frederick practiced his deep Texas dip Coronation bow for the audience.

BIGGER AND BIGGER

The Friendly Spot is an outdoor Texas ice house located in the Southtown part of San Antonio, owned by couple Jody Bailey Newman and Steve Newman, the first couple to sit on the royal Anchovy throne together. The seats of the ice house are sticky on this June morning, as we sit waiting for the fundraising ceremony to begin. The staff members of Black Effort Against the Threat of AIDS (BEAT AIDS) are already present, along with three college students. The director, Michelle Durham, stands up to receive an $80,000 check from Cornyation on behalf of her organization. For a smaller AIDS service organization like BEAT AIDS, this influx of funds helps them stay afloat and cover important operating expenses.[23] The director of the San Antonio AIDS Foundation (SAAF) is stuck in traffic and arrives late. He also remarks at the importance of the $80,000 check he receives on behalf of his organization, stating that it is more money than was raised internally by SAAF during the WEBB Party that year. Young women accept checks from the Robert Rehm Theatre Arts Scholarship for the performing arts from wheelchair-bound Robert Rehm, longtime Cornyation designer.

By the 2000s Cornyation had become a fundraising tour de force. Through the use of a volunteer crew and the creative selling of T-shirts, seats, tables, and advance tickets, Cornyation had become devoted to fundraising for San Antonio charities. And although almost all Fiesta events are fundraisers, Cornyation became remarkable for the amount of money it raised. Between 2000 and 2008 the show donated more than $500,000 to local charities, quadruple the amount it raised in the 1990s.[24] By the end of the 2000s Cornyation was raising more than $100,000 each year. In the 2010s these efforts were increased further as a number of Cornyation royalty figures began to fundraise independently in the months leading up to the show. Most of these funds were directed toward HIV/AIDS service organizations, although charities like Project Heart have also received more than $50,000 over time from the show.

The scale and focus of this fundraising is a source of pride for almost all designers and cast members. Many Cornyation performers brag that apart from the union stage crew who are hired for the show, "no one gets paid." All efforts are volunteer, and each skit raises its own funds to cover materials for the skit. According to Cornyation board member Jesse Mata, "They don't get paid—nobody gets paid for this, so you're donating your time, your money." "The designers who aren't so good at prolific fundraising come out of pocket for a lot of this stuff," Mata continued. "So these are people who really—who are, you know, great people, who are dedicated to doing something significant for the community."[25] Cornyation participants often contrast their fundraising with the expenses of other Fiesta events, pointing out they were less indulgent on extravagances like fancy medals and car entourages. One Cornyation board member remarked that "our royalty pays for their own parking," in stark comparison to the multicar entourage and police escort afforded other major Fiesta royalty.

LIFE AND DEATH AND EVERYTHING IN BETWEEN

The 2000s were also a period of great loss and tragedy for the Cornyation cast members and board members. The deaths of three Cornyation steadies— R. Cotham "Bob" Jolly, Danny Geisler, and Pat Wells—and the dramatic injury and death of longtime Cornyation designer Robert Rehm altered the course of the show.

Jolly had consistently steered the Cornyation ship with codirector Ray Chavez and had been the master of ceremonies in almost every show since 1982. His clever, rhyming scripts set the tone for the event. Designers and cast members recalled fondly his artistic talents, including his joy in making Christmas ornaments with his image on them. His death from heart disease at the age of seventy in 2007 stunned the cast and transformed the Cornyation board. The show memorialized him with a skit, medal, and pithy poem in the program.

Picture of Ray Chavez and Bob Jolly, undated.

ODE To: R. Cotham Jolly "Cornyation" 2007
1937 - 2007

We will remember Bob best for his:

R.: Rambunctious readings of ribald reports
                 his
C: Cerebral, and cutting, and cheeky retorts
O: Outrageous, outspoken, oratorical gems
T: Terrorist tactics, testimonial whims
H: Highbrow humor and harrassing puns
A: Astute, acerbic wit, always making fun
M: Mischievous, mercurial, Master of Silly
                 his
J: Jousting, and jawing, as jokes fly willy nilly
O: OUT-landish, OUT-spoken, "Don't be a bore"
L: Loquacious, long winded, light hearted lore
L: Laughing loudly at lunkheads, right from the start
Y: Yearly reminders he was yet Young at Heart!!

"Good night, sweet Bob...
And Cornucopias of Cornyation Characters
And Querulous Quarreling Queens
Sing thee to thy rest" ......
It is as Master of the Revels
We will remember you best.

And so "Bon Voyage", Jolly Robert
From each infamous friend
May they hail you in heaven
Where rowdy revels never end
Where Fiesta Queens rule
And Cornyation reigns Supreme
And the Empress is singing that "life is but a dream"

www.cornyation.org

Program in memorial to Bob Jolly, 2007.

Homemade medal for King Anchovy Debra Guerrero, designed by Danny Geisler.

Jolly's name still appears on the Cornyation programs as emeritus emcee/scriptwriter.

Longtime designer Danny Geisler, who was often called "Mister Danny Geisler," also passed away during this time. An eccentric visual artist whose art a reviewer once described as "accessorized worst-case scenarios,"[26] Geisler had been a designer for more than a decade. He was also known for his handmade invitations and Cornyation medals, including homemade medals for many Kings Anchovy. Geisler passed away in 2006 at the age of fifty-one. Protégée Leora Uribe, who had worked with Geisler at an arts organization called Say Sí, designed a memorial skit for her mentor the next year, and thereafter became a new regular female designer in the Cornyation ensemble.

During this same time period, longtime Cornyation designer Robert Rehm experienced a dramatic, life-changing accident. Rehm had been a director and teacher of theater arts for nine years at Thomas Jefferson High School. While rehearsing students for a play in 2005 he fell off the Jefferson stage into the orchestra pit; the accident left him paralyzed from the neck down. With a buoyant, determined spirit, Rehm rejoined the Cornyation crew in 2006 and continued designing with the assistance of a mouth-controlled computer and a cast of theater friends who helped him make costumes. The Cornyation board instituted the Robert Rehm Theatre Arts Scholarship in 2006 to support students in the performing arts. By the time of his death in 2015 Rehm had designed for twenty Cornyation shows.[27]

In 2016 the Cornyation cast faced another tough year of loss. New designer Mark Steckly died tragically in a car accident. Longtime Cornyation designer, stage manager, and self-proclaimed "Head Dominatrix" Pat Wells passed away suddenly in her home days before the 2016 show. On the same day John McBurney's lover of thirty-five years, Mike Marmontello, died.[28] Both Wells and Marmontello had participated in Cornyation for decades.

Designer Robert Rehm with his cast members at a cast party.

THE SHOW MUST GO ON

When Cornyation began in 1951, the organizers of the show could not have predicted it would become what it is today. The 2015 show of Cornyation marked the fiftieth year of the rule of King Anchovy—fifty years of duchesses in costumes, witty satire, dancing queens, entertainment, audience hijinks, hot glue burns, and biting humor. Over these fifty years, the organizers and performers of the show fundraised to support the infrastructure of art, theater, and health organizations; they criticized the status quo with biting commentary and satire; and they created a space for people from across the city to perform camp.

The content and structure of the show has changed dramatically since its start as a fundraiser for the San Antonio Little Theater during Fiesta; the mocking of the Coronation in the 1950s is radically different from skits that satirize celebrity culture and reality television in the 2010s. What has stayed consistent is the campy, corny satire that defines the show, and that is of course, just as with the very first Cornyation Court of the Cracked Salad Bowl, still cracked.

■ ■ ■

ACKNOWLEDGMENTS

It truly takes a village to write a book, and this book would not have been possible without an entire village of people letting me interview them, participate in Cornyation, and dig through their files.

First and foremost, this work would not have been possible without the support of Ray Chavez, who spent tireless hours explaining the show to me, letting me scan his files, and reading multiple drafts. The Cornyation Board—including Tom McKenzie, Elaine Wolff, Curt Slangal, Jesse Mata, Tinker Kochwelp, and Brad Braune—were critical in moving this project forward. Without Lori Hall, this project never would have gotten off the ground, as she saw the potential in it from day one. Without Christine Drennon, I may never have gone to the show or met Lori Hall. Pat Wells deserves extra thanks for tolerating me as a stage crew hand for a few years. This book was intellectually supported by colleagues Melissa Gohlke, Jason Burton Johnson, Michaele Haynes, and Laura Hernández-Ehrisman.

At Trinity University, the assistance of Caitlin Gallagher, John Dean Domingue, and Analicia Garcia was critical in conducting research for this project. At the last minute, Beatrice Roman helped in coordinating and selecting photographs. This research could not have been conducted without generous support from Trinity University Academic Affairs and the Murchison Summer Undergraduate Research Fellowship. Support from Trinity University Press was critical for purchasing copyright permissions for many of the photographs in this volume. The support of Tom Payton, the director of the press, and the enthusiasm and professionalism of Sarah Nawrocki, Burgin Streetman, and the rest of the press staff made this book come together. Anne Richmond Boston's beautiful design work was more amazing than I ever could have expected.

In the realm of archives, Tom Shelton at the Institute of Texan Culture knows more about the photographic history of San Antonio than anyone, and he was an enthusiastic supporter of this project. Gene Elder at the Happy Foundation was my co-conspirator in digging up San Antonio lesbian and gay history. Carolyn Weathers and John McBurney provided me with much of the photographic history of San Antonio lesbian and gay life. Without the support of Playhouse director Asia Ciaravino, I would not have found the Cornyation scripts from the 1950s and 1960s. The archival reorganization of the Playhouse archives by Katie Cueller, Stacey Connelly, and Amy Roberson made detailed analysis of these files possible. Melissa Gohlke fielded numerous random requests at the University of Texas San Antonio Special Collections. The Texana Collection at the San Antonio Public Library is an important, consistently underfunded resource that also made this project possible. The technical assistance of Pat Ulmann and her loan of a scanner were critical. Finally, Wayne Byall so patiently dug through piles of old scrapbooks and home movies to find photographs of his mother and one of the only recordings of the 1963 Cornyation.

So many people allowed me to dig through their photo files and to scan their documents, or processed photos for me, often with little or no remuneration. Michael Mehl and Al Rendon were generous in sharing their time, knowledge, and artistry. John McBurney spent hours with me digging through old photos of Cornyation and the Ponderosa and taught me much about the history of drag in San Antonio. Curt Slangal and Rene Roberts were always generous with their time and materials. Reuben Njaa and Michelle Davis readily gave consent for the use of their photographs in this project.

In my personal life, I thank the ongoing support of my wonderful people, including Angela Tarango, Vanessa Haupt, Jason Johnson, Holly Lindsey, Gale McCommons, J Mote, Angela McCaughery, David Dyson, Kellye Green, and Amy Hinsley. As always, I thank Kris Herzog and Bill Grindatti for being there.

Last but not least, thanks to the cast of Cornyation who let me sit and interview them for hours. Even if you are not mentioned in this book, you are an important part of this story. Some interviewees, like Debra Guerrero, went above and beyond the call of duty. Mark Steckley so generously recruited me to be his duchess for two years; thank you for overlooking my awkward attempts at dancing and costuming, Mark. You passed from this earth far too soon. His crew of Patrick, Chris, Tim, Enrique, Alberto, Grant, Stephen, and Joseph took such great care of me during the show. This book could not have been possible without Tim's wig donation.

CREDITS

Page x, courtesy of Sheryl Sculley

Pages xi, xvii, 12, 19, 20, 22, 26, 40, 49, 51, 52, 76, 84, 91, 98, and 111 (top), courtesy of the Institute of Texan Cultures

Pages xii, xxi, 7, 14, 28, 29, 41, 46, and 63 (left and right), courtesy of the Playhouse and the San Antonio Public Library Texana Collection

Pages xiii and 50, courtesy of Wayne Byall

Pages xv, xix (top and bottom), xxii (left and right), 121 (left and right), 123 (top left and top right), 124, 126, 127 (top), 132 (top), 136 (bottom), and 141, photography by Lauryn Farris

Page xvi, courtesy of the San Antonio Public Library Texana Collection

Pages xviii and 140, photography by Beatrice Roman

Pages xx, 79, 82, and 100, photography by Reuben Njaa

Pages xxiii, xxvii, 78, 83, 87, 89, 97, 107, and 108 (bottom), photography by Michael Mehl

Page 3 (left), courtesy of ZUMA and the *San Antonio Express-News*

Pages 3 (right), 8, 17, 31, 32, 34, 39, 43, 45, 61, 62, and 69, courtesy of the Playhouse

Page 5, Light Collection, courtesy of the Institute of Texan Cultures

Page 6, Zintgraff Studio Photograph Collection, courtesy of the University of Texas San Antonio Special Collections

Page 54, courtesy of Harlandale School District

Pages 55 and 56, courtesy of Carolyn Weathers and One Archives

Page 59, courtesy of the University of Texas San Antonio Special Collections

Pages 67, 103, 104, 108 (top), 111 (middle and bottom), 113, and 127 (bottom), photography by Al Rendon

Pages 70, 81, 101, 117, 129, 134, and 139 (bottom), courtesy of Ray Chavez

Pages 72 and 86, courtesy of the *Calendar*

Pages 74 (left and right), and 125, courtesy of John McBurney

Pages 92 and 93, courtesy of Cal Sumner

Pages 108 (middle), 123 (bottom), and 133, photography by Belinda Stanush

Page 114, courtesy of Ted Switzer; original cover photo by Michael Mehl

Page 132 (bottom), courtesy of Debra Guerrero

Page 135, photography by Amy L. Stone

Page 136 (top), photography by Marc Arevalo

Page 139 (top), courtesy of Curt Slangal

NOTES

Introduction

1   Lindsay Kastner, "A Super Cornyation," *San Antonio Express-News*, April 22, 2009, 01B.

2   Nancy Preyor-Johnson, "Fiesta's Cornyation Gives Charities a Reason to Celebrate," *San Antonio Express-News*, July 26, 2009, 03B.

3   Ibid.

4   Félix D. Almaráz, *Standing Room Only: A History of the San Antonio Little Theatre, 1912–1962* (Waco: Texian Press, 1964), 110.

5   "Two Kings Anchovy for Cornyation 2016," Out in SA, Dec. 9, 2015, http://outinsa.com /two-kings-anchovy-for-cornyation-2016.

6   For scholarship on festivals as a site of the carnivalesque, see Mikhail Bakhtin, *Rabelais and His World* (Bloomington: Indiana University Press, 1984), and Peter Stallybrass and Allon White, *The Politics and Poetics of Transgression* (London: Methuen Press, 1986). For scholarship on festivals as a site of racial exclusion see James Gill, *Lords of Misrule: Mardi Gras and the Politics of Race in New Orleans* (Jackson: University Press of Mississippi, 1997), and Sam Kinser, *Carnival, American Style: Mardi Gras at New Orleans and Mobile* (University of Chicago Press, 1990).

7   Stallybrass and White, *Politics and Poetics*, 4. Some of the most important debates about festivals have taken place in reaction to them. See Bakhtin, *Rabelais and His World*, and Stallybrass and White, *Politics and Poetics*.

8   Bakhtin, *Rabelais and His World*, 4; Stallybrass and White, *Politics and Poetics*.

9   Historical pageants like Fiesta and its Battle of the Flowers parade are common throughout the Southwest. For example, Santa Fe Fiesta is one of the longest-running city festivals in the United States.

10   Laura Hernández-Ehrisman, *Inventing the Fiesta City: Heritage and Carnival in San Antonio* (Albuquerque: University of New Mexico Press, 2008), chapter 4.

11   Monica Sassatelli, "Urban Festivals and the Cultural Public Sphere," in *Festivals and the Cultural Public Sphere*, ed. Liana Giorgi, Monica Sassatelli, and Gerard Delanty (London: Routledge, 2011), 12–28.

12   My research builds on the broader study of cultural citizenship, or belonging to a social entity larger than oneself and being acknowledged by that entity as a member. By emphasizing the cultural and social aspects of citizenship, this project theorizes about the complexity of marginalized groups' integration into urban communities. It answers a broader question about how one becomes an integrated member of a complex, multicultural society. For more on cultural citizenship, see Aihwa Ong, "Cultural Citizenship as Subject-Making: Immigrants Negotiate Racial and Cultural Boundaries in the United States," *Current Anthropology* 37 (1996): 737–62; Renato Rosaldo, "Cultural Citizenship and Educational Democracy," *Cultural Anthropology* 9 (1994): 402–11; Margaret R. Somers, *Genealogies of Citizenship: Markets, Statelessness, and the Right to Have Rights* (New York: Cambridge University Press, 2008); Charles Taylor, *Multiculturalism: Examining the Politics of Recognition*, edited by Amy Gutmann (Princeton University Press, 1994); and Iris Marion Young, *Justice and the Politics of Difference* (Princeton University Press, 1990).

13 Although I interviewed individuals who are lesbian, bisexual, and transgender who participate in Cornyation, the show is primarily shaped by a gay male aesthetic. Camp, as well, is territorially controlled by gay men. For more information, read Esther Newton, "Dick(Less) Tracy and the Homecoming Queen: Lesbian Power and Representation in Gay Male Cherry Grove," in *Margaret Mead Made Me Gay*, ed. Esther Newton (Durham, NC: Duke University Press, [1996] 2000), 63–89.

14 Mike Greenberg, "Court Jesters," *San Antonio Express-News*, April 23, 1997, 1G.

15 Scholars often argue that what happens during festivals is only a temporary subversion of the status quo or a release of energy that is sanctioned by social and political elites.

16 Quotations from the video of the 2014 Cornyation "Court of Festive Fetes and Frivolous Faux Pas," filmed by Farris Family Film and Photography.

17 For a good definition of camp, see Susan Sontag's 1964 essay, "Notes on Camp," in *Camp: Queer Aesthetics and the Performing Subject: A Reader*, ed. Fabio Cleto (Ann Arbor: University of Michigan Press, 1999), 53–65; see also Esther Newton, *Mother Camp: Female Impersonators in America* (University of Chicago Press, 1972).

18 See my argument on this in Amy L. Stone, "Crowning King Anchovy: Cold War Gay Visibility in San Antonio's Urban Festival," *Journal of the History of Sexuality* 25:2 (2016): 297–322.

Chapter 1: The 1950s

1 Russell Rodgers and Chips Utley, "Court of the Cracked Salad Bowl" script, 1951, box 10, Playhouse Archives, San Antonio, Texas (cited hereafter as Playhouse Archives).

2 Amy Freeman Lee (1914–2004) was a well-known watercolor artist who also wrote an art critic column for the local municipal newspaper. For more information on Lee, see the archive of her papers by Texas Archival Resources Online at www.lib.utexas.edu/taro /ttusw/00033/tsw-00033.html.

3 Michaele Haynes, *Dressing Up Debutantes: Pageantry and Glitz in Texas* (New York: Berg, 1998).

4 Hernández-Ehrisman, *Inventing the Fiesta City*, chapter 4.

5 Stone, "Crowning King Anchovy," 305–10.

6 Rogers Jr. and his two older brothers, the late Napier Rogers and Russell Hill Rogers, "developed the property their father, Wallace Rogers Sr., bought in 1947. The 7,500 acres Rogers Sr. bought were part of the Stowers Ranch holdings owned by George Arthur Stowers, a Georgia-born furniture store owner who died in 1917." The Shavano Park population grew from 167 in 1956 to 1,709 in 1990. See Carmina Danini, "Shavano Park Co-developer Rogers Dies," *San Antonio Express-News*, May 24, 2000, 6B.

7 SALT was founded in 1912 by Sarah Barton Bindley and was incorporated in 1927. For a history of SALT see Almaráz, *Standing Room Only*.

8 The Carolina Playmakers, *Patience* program, 1941, box 10, Playhouse Archives.

9 Russell Rogers is now more commonly referred to as Russell Hill Rogers. Rogers bequeathed his money to the Russell Hill Rogers Fund for the Arts, a major financial supporter of arts buildings and programs in San Antonio.

10 Oral History of John Palmer Leeper, conducted by John Lindquist, August 1996. Courtesy of the McNay Art Museum Archives.

11   Interview with Jamie Maverick by author and John Dean Domingue, June 21, 2012; similar sentiments were reported in interviews with four other arts patrons whose interviews are confidential.

12   Ray Chavez, "Conversation between Joe Salek, Ray Chavez, and Russell Rogers," *Forum*, March/April 1986, 21. It is consequential that Salek lived in King William, a neighborhood south of the San Antonio downtown; King William went through an urban renaissance in the 1960s thanks to the influx of creative professionals like Salek. According to a 1983 survey of the gay population of the city, about one-third of gay men lived in the zip codes for the King William neighborhood. For more on King William history, see "History," King William Association, www.ourkwa.org/about-us/history.html. For more on the 1983 survey, see Melissa Ann Gohlke, "Out in Alamo City: Revealing San Antonio's Gay and Lesbian Past, World War II to the 1990s" (master's thesis, University of Texas San Antonio, 2012).

13   Coronation of the Queen of the Order of the Alamo Program, Court of Islands, 1950, box 10, Playhouse Archives.

14   Chavez, "Conversation between Joe Salek, Ray Chavez, and Russell Rogers," 21.

15   Ibid., 21.

16   Gerald Ashford, "Little Theater Players Shine in Presenting 'Mr. Roberts,'" *San Antonio Express-News*, Jan. 28, 1954, 16A; "PTA Sets Program," *San Antonio Light*, March 25, 1951, 4-C.

17   Miriam McGary, "Pilon," *San Antonio Light*, April 20, 1951, 5-1.

18   Margaret Clark, "Fiesta Frolic at La Villita Huge Success," *San Antonio Light*, April 18, 1951, C1.

19   McGary, "Pilon," 5-1.

20   Clark, "Fiesta Frolic at La Villita a Huge Success," C1.

21   Gerald Ashford, "6,000 Go Mad at Cornyation," *San Antonio Express-News*, April 22, 1954, 1A, 3A.

22   "Cornyation Again Makes Big Hit," *San Antonio Express-News*, April 20, 1955, 4A.

23   David Roberts, "Little Theatre Satire Royally Pokes Fun at Titles," *San Antonio Light*, April 20, 1955, 2.

24   Bill Reddell, "Old Days Live in La Villita," *San Antonio Express-News*, April 18, 1955, 4A.

25   Carrington, a native Virginian, moved to Texas as a young man. His deep interest in southern traditions and chivalry, along with his involvement in promoting the Battle of the Flowers parade, motivated his creation of the Order of the Alamo with a group of friends. See Haynes, *Dressing Up Debutantes*, 38.

26   Ibid., 17.

27   Hernández-Ehrisman, *Inventing the Fiesta City*, 144–45.

28   Ibid.

29   Haynes, *Dressing Up Debutantes*, 42.

30   Ibid.

31   "Political Satire on Fiesta Floats," *San Antonio Express-News*, April 23, 1915.

32   "Gale of Mirth Is Created by Mock Pageant," *San Antonio Light*, April 22, 1917, 7.

33   Brock Thompson, *The Un-Natural State: Arkansas and the Queer South* (Fayetteville: University of Arkansas Press, 2010), 19.

34   Melissa Gohlke, "Womanless Wedding," *The Top Shelf: A Blog about Special Collections at the UTSA Libraries*, last modified Sept. 17, 2012, https://utsalibrariestopshelf.wordpress.com/2012/09/17/womanless-wedding/.

35   "Conopians Show How Queen Crowned," *San Antonio Express-News Magazine*, May 9, 1925, 29.

36   Hernández-Ehrisman, *Inventing the Fiesta City*, 103.
37   Ibid., 106.
38   Ibid., 110.
39   Ibid., 104.
40   David Ralph Johnson, John A. Booth, and Richard J. Harris, *The Politics of San Antonio: Community, Progress, and Power* (Lincoln: University of Nebraska Press, 1983).
41   Hernández-Ehrisman, *Inventing the Fiesta City*, 103.
42   Ibid., 111.
43   Ibid., 114–15.
44   Ibid., 103.
45   Ibid., 99.
46   See Lewis F. Fisher, *Saving San Antonio: The Precarious Preservation of a Heritage* (Lubbock: Texas Tech University Press, 1996).
47   Hernández-Ehrisman, *Inventing the Fiesta City*, 99.
48   Ibid., chapter 3.
49   Ibid., 98.
50   Ibid., 100–101.
51   "Arneson River Theater in San Antonio," City-Data.com, www.city-data.com/articles /Arneson-River-Theater-in-San-Antonio.html.
52   "How did the term corny develop," Quora, www.quora.com/How-did-the-term-corny-develop.
53   Almaráz, *Standing Room Only*, 97.
54   The Maverick family is a part of the heritage elite of San Antonio, descendants of Samuel Augustus Maverick, a rancher known for refusing to brand his cattle. The term "maverick" derives from this family's name. John Schwartz, "Who You Callin' a Maverick?," *New York Times*, Oct. 4, 2008, www.nytimes.com/2008/10/05/weekinreview/05schwartz.html.
55   Maury Maverick Jr. was known in Texas as a "firebrand civil libertarian and lawyer who defended draft resisters, atheists and others scorned by society"; Schwartz, "Who You Callin' a Maverick?" See also Maury Maverick and Allan O. Kownslar, *Texas Iconoclast, Maury Maverick Jr.* (Fort Worth: Texas Christian University Press, 1997).
56   K. Barnett Shaw (1909–2001) was a jeweler when he was King Anchovy but later became a Dallas Theater Center company member well-known for his English translations of French plays. See Tom Sime, "K. Barnett Shaw—Dallas actor, playwright, songwriter," *Dallas Morning News*, Aug. 24, 2001, 33A.
57   Charles Grace was a member of the Bexar County Democratic Coalition and was well-known as a liberal Democrat in San Antonio. His election as county judge was one of the major accomplishments of the coalition. Rodolfo Rosales, *The Illusion of Inclusion: The Untold Political Story of San Antonio* (Austin: University of Texas Press, 2000), 93.
58   The selection process for empresses in the early days of the show is unclear; interviews and archival data do not shed much light.
59   McGary, "Pilon," 5-1.
60   "Alice Naylor," Ask Art, www.askart.com/artist/Alice_Stephenson_Naylor/121409/Alice _Stephenson_Naylor.aspx.
61   The planning and building of the San Antonio Expressway (now Highway 281) made it "Texas's most controversial freeway" due to the strength of the opposition from various interest

groups, including strong opposition led by the San Antonio Conservation Society. "The San Antonio North Expressway Study, June 1971," Texas Freeway, last modified Aug. 6, 2001, www .texasfreeway.com/sanantonio/historic/281_1971_study/281_1971_study.shtml.

62 Moursund also coauthored the 1958 "Court of Outer Space" script with John Gilmore, and Lois Burkhalter coauthored the political 1959 script for "The Court of Sport of Sports: The Political Game in San Antonio" with her boss, Leeper.

63 "Cornyation Top Attraction at La Villita," *San Antonio Express-News*, 1953, Cornyation Files, San Antonio Public Library Texana Collection (hereafter Texana Collection).

64 Chavez, "Conversation between Joe Salek, Ray Chavez, and Russell Rogers," 21.

65 Joske's was a major department store chain that originated in San Antonio. "Joske's," Texas State Historical Association, https://tshaonline.org/handbook/online/articles/dhjqn.

66 "Texas Glamour: Les Wilks Design Digital Archive," Gateway to Women's History, Texas Woman's University, http://twudigital.contentdm.oclc.org/cdm/landingpage/collection /p15075coll1.

67 "Obituary: P. J. Allen," *Lockhart Post Register*, May 25, 2006, post-register.com.

68 Bill Reily, interview with author, July 13, 2012.

69 "Alonzo obituary," MySA.com, www.legacy.com/obituaries/sanantonio/obituary.aspx?n= alonzo&pid=92233893.

70 See Gohlke, "Out in Alamo City," for information on Travis Park as a center of gay sexual activity.

71 Paul Thompson, "Top of the News," *Sunday Express and News*, Feb. 14, 1960, 1A.

72 Information retrieved from the 1940 Census.

73 "Obituary: P. J. Allen."

74 "Obituary: Jud Davis," *MySA*, June 29, 2013, http://www.legacy.com/obituaries/sanantonio /obituary.aspx?pid=165575674.

75 Elaine Kaufman, interview with author, July 17, 2012.

76 Allan Berube, *Coming Out under Fire: The History of Gay Men and Women in World War II* (Chapel Hill: University of North Carolina Press, 2010), 87; Craig M. Loftin, *Masked Voices: Gay Men and Lesbians in Cold War America* (Albany: SUNY Press, 2012), 203–22; Martin Meeker, *Contacts Desired: Gay and Lesbian Communications and Community, 1940s–1970s* (University of Chicago Press, 2006), 8.

77 See Loftin, *Masked Voices*.

78 Although most gay men and lesbians had to remain "masked" in the work world and public life, there were two groups of individuals who were "unmasked" about their sexuality. According to Esther Newton in her book *Mother Camp*, men and women who worked in the gay world, as bar owners, bartenders, or performers, were exempt from this masking. The second group consisted of gay men and lesbians working in non-gender-normative occupations; for example, male hairdressers and window decorators and female construction workers may have been assumed to be gay and thus had more freedom in public life. Scholars call these "occupational strategies" or "gay ghetto" occupations. M. V. Badgett and Mary C. King, "Lesbian and Gay Occupational Strategies," in *Homo Economics: Capitalism, Community, and Lesbian and Gay Life*, ed. Amy Gluckman and Betsy Reed (New York: Routledge, 1997), 73–86.

79 Stone, "Crowning King Anchovy," 317.

80 See David K. Johnson, *The Lavender Scare: The Cold War Persecution of Gays and Lesbians in the Federal Government* (University of Chicago Press, 2009).

81 Vito Russo, *The Celluloid Closet* (New York: Harper & Row, 1987); Meeker, *Contacts Desired.*

82 Haynes, *Dressing Up Debutantes*, 164–66.

83 Ibid., 17.

84 See Phyllis Chesler, *Women and Madness* (New York: Palgrave Macmillan, 1989); Deborah Findlay, "The Good, the Normal and the Healthy: The Social Construction of Medical Knowledge about Women," *Canadian Journal of Sociology* (1993): 115–35.

85 Order of the Alamo, Coronation program, Court of Islands, 1950, Playhouse Archives.

86 Program for Court of Allergies, 1952, box 10, Playhouse Archives; Program for Court of Human Annoyances, 1957, box 10, Playhouse Archives.

87 David Roberts, "Little Theatre Satire Royally Pokes Fun at Titles," *San Antonio Light*, April 20, 1955, 2.

88 Program for Court of the Glorified Barnyard, 1955, box 10, Playhouse Archives.

89 Ibid.

90 Haynes, *Dressing Up Debutantes*, 3–4.

91 Ibid., 98.

92 Ibid., 104.

93 Chavez, "Conversation between Joe Salek, Ray Chavez, and Russell Rogers."

94 Allison Bergwin Fenton, phone interview with author, July 10, 2012.

95 "'Night' Draws Gay Throng," *San Antonio Express-News*, April 24, 1952, 5.

96 Chavez, "Conversation between Joe Salek, Ray Chavez, and Russell Rogers."

97 Almaráz, *Standing Room Only*, 102.

98 Newspaper clipping, "A Letter to Bessie: And Now Siesta," undated, SALT Theatre Files, Texana Collection.

99 "Cornyation Top Attraction at La Villita."

100 McGary, "Pilon," 5-1.

101 Robert Cotham Jolly, interview with Michaele Haynes, undated. Courtesy of Michaele Haynes.

102 Jan Bradley, "Post-Script: Cornyation under the Fence," *San Antonio Express-News*, April 22, 1954, 1B.

103 Hal Wingo, "Ole S.A. Was Never Like This: Big Can of Sardines," *San Antonio Light*, April 19, 1961, 1A.

104 Betty Scheibl, "Fiesta Madness Hits Bugsy Peak at 'Court,'" *San Antonio Light*, April 22, 1954, 32.

105 Russell Rogers, "The Cornyation Cast Check," 1952, box 10, Playhouse Archives.

106 "Just for Fun," *San Antonio Express-News Magazine*, April 19, 1953, 12.

107 "Cornyation Again Makes Big Hit," *San Antonio Express-News*, April 20, 1955, 4A.

108 "Alamo Almanac," *San Antonio Express-News*, April 17, 1955, 1G.

109 Chavez, "Conversation between Joe Salek, Ray Chavez, and Russell Rogers."

110 Roy Shuptrine, phone interview with author, June 18, 2012.

111 Claudia Poff, "This One's Just for Fun," *San Antonio Express-News Magazine*, April 18, 1954, 3.

Chapter 2: The 1960s

1   Lois Burkhalter and John Palmer Leeper, "Court of Broken Traditions" script, 1960, box 10, Playhouse Archives.
2   Ibid.
3   Ibid.
4   "Fiesta Fun: 'Cornyation,'" *San Antonio Express-News*, April 20, 1960, Box OM11. Fiesta San Antonio Commission Records, 1898, 1926–2005, MS 30, University of Texas at San Antonio Libraries Special Collections (hereafter Fiesta UTSA Collection).
5   Bill Freeman, "I've Been Told," *San Antonio Express-News*, April 26, 1953, 3B.
6   "Cornyation Top Attraction at La Villita," *San Antonio Express-News*, 1953, Cornyation Files, Texana Collection.
7   Ibid.
8   "Cornyation Again Makes Big Hit," *San Antonio Express-News*, April 20, 1955, 4A.
9   Gerald Ashford, "How to Improve Fiesta," *San Antonio Express-News*, April 23, 1956, 4A.
10 Ibid., 102.
11 Chavez, "Conversation between Joe Salek, Ray Chavez, and Russell Rogers."
12 Ann Moursund Lee and John Gilmore, "Court of Outer Space" script, 1958, box 10, Playhouse Archives.
13 Ibid.
14 See Rosales, *The Illusion of Inclusion*.
15 Ibid.
16 Ibid.
17 Hernández-Ehrisman, *Inventing the Fiesta City*.
18 Jim Collins, phone interview with author, July 6, 2012.
19 Philip Core, "From Camp: The Lie That Tells the Truth," in *Camp: Queer Aesthetics and the Performing Subject: A Reader, ed.* Fabio Cleto (Ann Arbor: University of Michigan Press, 1999), 80–87, 81.
20 Elaine Kaufman, interview with author, July 17, 2012.
21 Johnson, *The Lavender Scare*, 2–3.
22 Pete Daniel, *Lost Revolutions: The South in the 1950s* (Chapel Hill: University of North Carolina Press, 2000).
23 Daniel, *Lost Revolutions*.
24 Kristin Luker, *When Sex Goes to School: Warring Views on Sex—and Sex Education—since the Sixties* (New York: W. W. Norton, 2007), chapter 3.
25 Bill Carter, interview with author and John Dean Domingue, June 22, 2012.
26 Burkhalter and Leeper, "Court of Broken Traditions" script.
27 Lee and Gilmore, "Court of Outer Space" script.
28 Ibid.
29 George Chauncey, *Gay New York: Gender, Urban Culture, and the Making of the Gay Male World, 1890–1940* (New York: Basic Books, 1994), 288.
30 Information from a 1963 home movie of Cornyation Fiesta Court of Civil and Uncivil Projects, courtesy of Wayne Byall.

31   Ken Maples and Bill Robinson, "Fiesta Court of Civil and Uncivil Projects" script, 1963, Playhouse Archives.

32   Harlandale High School yearbooks, 1951 and 1957 editions, courtesy of Harlandale School District.

33   Gohlke, "Out in Alamo City," 32.

34   Ibid.

35   Ibid.; Bill Carter, interview with the author and John Dean Domingue.

36   John Howard, in his introduction to *Carryin' On in the Gay and Lesbian South* (New York University Press, 1997), suggests that queer southerners have a history of going out into the country for sexual freedom and exploration.

37   There were actually three bars that were referred to as the Country—a bar in the early 1960s owned by two lesbians out in a rural area; Paul's Grove; and a bar in downtown San Antonio called the San Antonio Country owned by Hap Veltman in the 1970s. Gohlke, "Out in Alamo City"; personal communication with Carolyn Weathers.

38   Gene Elder, interview with the author, Feb. 24, 2012.

39   This kind of coded language was common in the 1950s and 1960s. See Chauncey, *Gay New York*.

40   Same-sex dancing was not allowed in bars within the city limits.

41   Carolyn Weathers, "Cheers Everybody!," Mazer Lesbian Archive, http://mazerlesbianarchives .crewnoble.com/story_6.html.

42   Ibid.

43   Carolyn Weathers, e-mail to author, Sept. 11, 2013.

44   The Western Parade was a smaller Fiesta parade that existed in the 1960s.

45   Script of Cornyation drag show, 1963, courtesy of Carolyn Weathers.

46   Ibid.

47   Hernández-Ehrisman, *Inventing the Fiesta City*.

48   Script of Cornyation drag show, 1963.

49   Chavez, "Conversation between Joe Salek, Ray Chavez, and Russell Rogers."

50   Ibid.

51   San Antonio Little Theatre Board of Directors Meeting Minutes, Feb. 17, 1965, unknown box, Playhouse Archives.

52   Letter from Padgitt and Weincek to Salek, Feb. 12, 1965, box 10, Playhouse Archives.

53   John Shown, "Some Call It Porn, but It's Mostly Corn," *San Antonio Express-News* magazine, April 17, 1983, 83.

54   Letter from Gene Brown to Joe Salek, Feb. 18, 1965, box 10, Playhouse Archives.

55   Letter from Terrill Hills Mayor, Harold M. Scherr to Mrs. Padgitt, Feb. 17, 1965, box 10, Playhouse Archives.

56   Letter from SALT Board to Padgitt and Weincek, undated, box 10, Playhouse Archives.

57   Ibid.

58   Editorial, "Fiesta Event Made Better," *San Antonio Express-News*, Feb. 21, 1965, 6H.

59   This is an older use of the word "gay" to mean "festive" or "fun."

60   Glenn Tucker, "Why Dethrone Cornyation?," *San Antonio Express-News*, Feb. 21, 1965, 11G.

61   Kenneth Maples, "Cornyation Slash Protested," letter to the editor, *San Antonio Express-News*, Feb. 23, 1965.

62 San Antonio Little Theater, Board of Directors meeting minutes, Feb. 17, 1965, Playhouse Archives.

63 Ibid.

64 Letter to Mr. Joe Salek from the San Antonio Fiesta Commission, Inc., March 5, 1965, box 10, Playhouse Archives.

65 Betty Jarman and Ted Fredricks, "Court of Great Society" script, 1965, box 10, Playhouse Archives.

66 "HemisFair '68," *Wikipedia*, https://en.wikipedia.org/wiki/HemisFair_%2768.

67 SALT Board of Trustees, meeting minutes, Nov. 17, 1965, box 10, Playhouse Archives.

Chapter 3: The 1980s

1 R. Cotham Jolly, "Twelve Dames of Christmas" script, 1985, Cornyation Archives as held by Ray Chavez (hereafter Cornyation Archives).

2 Ashlee Simmons, "History of the Fairmount Hotel in San Antonio," *USA Today*, http://traveltips .usatoday.com/history-fairmount-hotel-san-antonio-tx-21461.html.

3 Ibid.

4 "Floating Tacos, Dancing Nachos," *San Antonio Express-News,* April 20, 1974, 15A.

5 Unknown author, "Court of Disco" script, 1979, box 10, Playhouse Archives.

6 Ray Chavez, interview with author.

7 See Hernández-Ehrisman, *Inventing the Fiesta City*, for an authoritative account of the diversification of Fiesta. LULAC had created El Rey Feo in 1947 as the chief fundraiser for their scholarship program.

8 Rosales, *The Illusion of Inclusion*, 143.

9 Ibid., 194.

10 For a history of Stonewall, see David Carter, *Stonewall: The Riots That Sparked the Gay Revolution* (New York: Macmillan, 2005) and Elizabeth A. Armstrong and Suzanna M. Crage, "Movements and Memory: The Making of the Stonewall Myth," *American Sociological Review* 71:5 (2006): 724–51. For a history of gay liberation, see John D'Emilio, *Sexual Politics, Sexual Communities* (University of Chicago Press, 1998).

11 D'Emilio, *Sexual Politics, Sexual Communities*.

12 Fred Fejes, *Gay Rights and Moral Panic* (New York: Palgrave Macmillan, 2008); Tina Fetner, *How the Religious Right Shaped Lesbian and Gay Activism* (Minneapolis: University of Minnesota Press, 2008).

13 Gohlke, "Out in Alamo City," 55.

14 Ibid. John McBurney, interview with author, Nov. 9, 2012.

15 Beatrice Roman, "Country Days and Drag Nights on the South Side," *Out in SA*, July 12, 2015, http://outinsa.com/country-days-and-drag-nights-on-the-south-side.

16 Sarah Fisch, "The Visionary," *San Antonio Current*, Nov. 5, 2008, www.sacurrent.com /sanantonio/the-visionary/Content?oid=2284908.

17 See Gene Elder's play "Off Limits" for the authoritative account of the military trial.

18 Gohlke, "Out in Alamo City."

19 Ray Chavez, interview with author, Aug. 5, 2014.

20　Melissa Gohlke, "The John Shown Collection—A New Addition to UTSA Special Collections," The Top Shelf: A Blog about Special Collections at the UTSA Libraries, last modified Aug. 11, 2014, https://utsalibrariestopshelf.wordpress.com/2014/08/11/the-john-shown -collection-a-new-addition-to-utsa-special-collections.

21　"Sterling Houston," *Wikipedia*, last modified May 15, 2016, https://en.wikipedia.org/wiki /Sterling_Houston.

22　Kevin Johnson, "Cornyation Shows Off Tongue-in-Cheek Royalty," *San Antonio Light*, April 21, 1982, 7A.

23　Brad Braune, interview with author, June 29, 2012.

24　R. Cotham Jolly, "Broadway Musicals That Never Were" script, 1987, Cornyation Archives.

25　Ed Conroe, "Cornyation Jabs Fiesta Pomp," *San Antonio Express-News*, April 23, 1987, 4-D; Rosales, *The Illusion of Inclusion*, 152–56.

26　This line refers to the SeaWorld building contract and Bernardo Eureste, longtime San Antonio politician.

27　Yolanda Vera was the second Chicana city council member, elected in 1985. Rosales, *The Illusion of Inclusion*, 165.

28　This is a reference to Henry Cisneros, longtime city politician and the first Hispanic mayor of San Antonio.

29　C. A. Stubbs was a tax protestor and COPS opponent who tried to launch a government spending cap referendum in San Antonio. Peter Applebome, "In San Antonio, Officials Don't Laugh at Tax Fighter These Days," *New York Times*, May 11, 1986, www.nytimes .com/1986/05/11/us/in-san-antonio-officials-don-t-laugh-at-tax-fighter-these-days.html.

30　Weir Labatt was a replacement for city councilman Van Henry Archer, who died in office. Rosales, *The Illusion of Inclusion*, 194.

31　Jolly, "Broadway Musicals That Never Were" script.

32　"Fiesta Cornyation to Highlight Fiesta Week," *Artists Alliance Revue*, April 1983, unknown page, Cornyation Files, Happy Foundation Archives.

33　Lila Cockrell was the first woman elected mayor in San Antonio; she first served from 1975 to 1981. See Rosales, *The Illusion of Inclusion*, 142.

34　R. Cotham Jolly, "Court of Mythology" script, 1989, Cornyation Archives.

35　R. Cotham Jolly, "Court of Vacuous Video Vertigo" script, 1988, Cornyation Archives.

36　Randy Shilts, *And the Band Played On: People, Politics, and the AIDS Epidemic* (New York: St. Martin's, 1987).

37　Brad Braune, interview with author, June 29, 2012.

38　John Shown, "Academy of Surplus Awards" script, 1984, Cornyation Archives.

39　Ibid.

40　Esther Wu, "Cornyation Proves Some Like It Haute," *San Antonio Express-News*, April 20, 1983, 1C.

41　Tom McKenzie, interview with author, June 11, 2013.

42　Ibid.

43　Brad Braune, interview with author, June 29, 2012.

44　Curt Slangal, interview with author, Feb. 27, 2013.

45　"Resurrected Cornyation Pokes Fun at Rival," *San Antonio Express-News*, April 21, 1982, 1C.

46　Wu, "Cornyation Proves Some Like It Haute," 1C.

47   Susan Yerkes, "Dramatic Coronation and Cornyation Alternative," *San Antonio Express-News*, April 21, 1988, B1.

48   Cornyation Foundation, Inc., Board Meeting Minutes, March 7, 2000, Cornyation Archives.

49   Letter from Arthur Veltman Jr. to David Barnett, Executive Director of the San Antonio Fiesta Commission, Inc., Dec. 21, 1981, box 10, Playhouse Archives.

50   Letter from David Burnett Jr. to Arthur Veltman Jr., Jan. 7, 1982, box 10, Playhouse Archives.

51   The official Fiesta royalty include Queen of the Order of the Alamo, King Antonio, El Rey Feo, Miss Fiesta, Miss San Antonio the Queen of Soul, the Charro Queen, the teenage Queen, and the Reina de la Feria de las Flores. The unofficial royalty recognized in 1998 include King Anchovy, the Fiesta Hat King, and the Queen of the Piñatas. See Cal Sumner, "The Fiesta Hat of the Fiesta Hat King of San Antonio," revised Oct. 21, 2013, author's collection.

52   Cal Sumner, interview with author, May 15, 2014.

53   Ibid.

54   Sarah Fisch, "The Visionary," *San Antonio Current*, Nov. 5, 2008, www.sacurrent.com /sanantonio/the-visionary/Content?oid=2284908.

Chapter 4: The 1990s

1   Haynes, *Dressing Up Debutantes*.

2   R. Cotham Jolly, "Court of Courts" script, 1990, Cornyation Archives.

3   Ibid.

4   Taddy McAllister was the granddaughter of former San Antonio mayor Walter McAllister Jr. According to an interviewee, McAllister launched a noise ordinance in 1990. The regulation of gay bars and public parks by the military police is documented in Gohlke, "Out in Alamo City."

5   See Fetner, *How the Religious Right Shaped*, 105–6.

6   "Kimberly of the House of Corbin," *San Antonio Express-News*, April 26, 1990, B2.

7   "After 25 Years of Lampooning Fiesta Pomp and Pageantry—Cornyation," *San Antonio Express-News*, April 24, 1990.

8   Dan R. Goddard, "Wayne Elkins' Life, Death Touched So Many," *San Antonio Express-News* Sunday edition, March 25, 1990, https://www.satheatre.com/extras/17-memorials/120 -wayne-k-elkins-march-11-1990.html.

9   Pat Wells, interview with author, July 11, 2013.

10   This description is from watching video footage of multiple 1990s shows. Courtesy of the Happy Foundation.

11   Pat Wells, interview with author.

12   All interviews conducted by the author's research assistant Analicia Garcia in the summer of 2013.

13   Robert Wynne, "Annual Cornyation Marks Fiesta's Funkiest Royal-Romping Activities," *San Antonio Light*, April 22, 1992, H1.

14   Ibid.

15   Rick Casey, "Fiesta Family Values: Lynda's Tight Leather," *San Antonio Express-News*, April 28, 1996, accessed through Access World News Newsbank.

16   In the 1990s Texas state representative Jerry Beauchamp proposed that the control over the Alamo grounds be transferred from the Daughters of the Republic of Texas (DRT) to the Texas Parks and Wildlife Department, a proposal that was supported by minority legislators disgruntled by controversy over the DRT's finances and anti-Mexican sentiments in representations of the Alamo. Ultimately, DRT retained control over the historic landmark. See "Alamo Mission in San Antonio," *Wikipedia*, last modified on May 20, 1996, https://en.wikipedia.org/wiki/Alamo_Mission_in_San_Antonio#Ownership_dispute.

17   Pat Wells, interview with author.

18   R. Cotham Jolly, Court of the Blazing Sun script, 1993, Cornyation Archives.

19   Hernández-Ehrisman, *Inventing the Fiesta City*, chapter 5.

20   Rick Casey, "The Real, True Rey Feo Is No King Antonio Wannabe," *San Antonio Express-News*, April 18, 1993, 5A.

21   Ron Bechtol, "Anchovy Acceptance Comes from Years of Experimenting," *San Antonio Light*, April 22, 1992, H6.

22   Fetner, *How the Religious Right Shaped*, chapter 6.

23   Suzanna Danuta Walters, *All the Rage: The Story of Gay Visibility in America* (University of Chicago Press, 2003).

24   See Fetner, *How the Religious Right Shaped*, chapter 6. The full name of the policy is "Don't Ask, Don't Tell, Don't Pursue," but it's most commonly known as "Don't Ask, Don't Tell."

25   Diane Windeler, "Few Subjects Escape Cornyation Spoofs," *San Antonio Express-News*, April 22, 1993, 3D.

26   R. Cotham Jolly, "Court of the Blazing Sun" script, 1993, Cornyation Archives.

27   Urvashi Vaid, *Virtual Equality: The Mainstreaming of Gay and Lesbian Liberation* (New York: Anchor, 2015).

28   Kathy Lowry, "The Purple Passion of Sandra Cisneros," *Texas Monthly*, October 1997, www.texasmonthly.com/articles/the-purple-passion-of-sandra-cisneros.

29   Pat Wells, interview with author.

30   "Chartreuse Couch," interview of Susan Yerkes by Gene Elder, e-mail from Gene Elder, Jan. 6, 2014.

31   Brad Braune, interview with author.

32   "Funky, 'Family' Float Flouts Fiesta Flambeau," *San Antonio Marquise*, June 1997, 5.

33   Ibid.

34   "About Arts for Life," *San Antonio Marquise*, July 1, 1993, 4.

35   E-mail from Fiesta Cornyation, Inc., to Majestic Theatre Management, June 7, 2000, Cornyation Archives.

36   "Mission and Philosophy," San Antonio AIDS Foundation, accessed May 1, 2015, www.sanantonioaids.org/about/mission-and-philosophy1.

37   Tom McKenzie, interview with author, June 11, 2013.

38   Bill Davis, interview with author, June 28, 2012.

39   Randy Bear, interview with author, December 18, 2013.

40   Ibid.

Chapter 5: The 2000s and 2010s

1   This information is my own observations from participating in the stage crew in 2012.
2   "Cornyation 2004—Michael Jackson in Neverland," filmed April 2004, YouTube, 9:01. Posted July 2009, www.youtube.com/watch?v=m6PNNz3WGDU.
3   Pat Wells, interview with author.
4   The show organizers have allowed at least one transgender woman to be an empress.
5   "Beauty Queen in 'Tacos' Suit: 'I'm Still the Same Weight,'" *Today.com*, updated Feb. 12, 2011, http://www.today.com/id/41510482/ns/today-today_style/t/beauty-queen-tacos-suit-im -still-same-weight/#.V5JLd6JlyL0.
6   Amy Dorsett, "Battle of the Flours," *San Antonio Express-News*, April 24, 2003, 1B, 8B.
7   Hector Saldana, "Cornyation Takes Digs at Decades of Decadence," *San Antonio Express-News*, April 27, 2000, 3F.
8   Ibid.
9   Annette Hill, *Reality TV: Audiences and Popular Factual Television* (New York: Psychology Press, 2005).
10   Robert Crowe, "Cornyation Is as Corny, Fun as Ever," *San Antonio Express-News*, April 24, 2008, 08B.
11   John McBurney, interview with author.
12   Robert Rehm, interview with author, June 19, 2012.
13   Albatross, "Tortilla Tossing Missed," *Strange in San Antonio*, April 27, 2006, http://strange sanantonio.blogspot.com/2006/04/tortilla-tossing-missed.html.
14   Jesse Mata, interview with author, March 13, 2013.
15   Cornyation Standards for Designers, Cast and Crew, 2006, Cornyation Archives.
16   Haynes, *Dressing Up Debutantes*, 145.
17   Saldana, "Cornyation Takes Digs at Decades of Decadence."
18   For more information on Project Fiesta, see www.projectfiesta.com. Project Fiesta, incidentally, takes place at the same "Compound" that Dan and Harry used in the 1990s. Fiesta Frenzy began in 1999 as a cabaret night to raise funds for a fledgling effort at creating the first San Antonio LGBT Community Center. For more information see *QSanAntonio*, "Fiesta Frenzy to Benefit Theater Arts Students," April 17, 2017, http://qsanantonio.com /frenzy14.html. Fiesta Madness ended in 2006; the event included a drag contest for Miss Fiesta Madness. All information about Fiesta Madness came from Mark Steckly and Stephen Turner.
19   For more information on the Esperanza Peace and Justice Center, see www.esperanza center.org. I learned about the Fiesta medals while following the center on Facebook.
20   Jeanie Tavitas-Williams, "Meet Some Fiesta Royalty," *San Antonio Express-News*, April 21, 2002, 10J.
21   Saldana, "Cornyation Takes Digs at Decades of Decadence."
22   Pat Wells, interview with author.
23   Michelle Durham, interview with author and Rosa Olivares, July 1, 2014.
24   Nancy Preyor-Johnson, "Fiesta's Cornyation Gives Charities a Reason to Celebrate," *San Antonio Express-News*, July 26, 2009, 03B.
25   Jesse Mata, interview with author.

26   Elaine Wolff, "Arts Danny Geisler's New World," Nov. 4, 2005, *San Antonio Current*, www.sa
      current.com/sanantonio/arts-danny-geislers-new-world/Content?oid=2275084.

27   Deborah Martin, "S.A. Theatre Mainstay Rehm Dies," *San Antonio Express-News*, Jan. 6, 2015,
      www.mysanantonio.com/entertainment/music-stage/article/S-A-theater-mainstay-Rehm
      -dies-5994745.php.

28   "Hot Glue & Duct Tape: John McBurney's Rasquache Aesthetic," April 16, 2016, http://
      outinsa.com/hot-glue-duct-tape-john-mcburneys-rasquache-aesthetic.

Notes

INDEX

Index

Amy Stone is an associate professor of sociology and anthropology at Trinity University. She is the author of *Gay Rights at the Ballot Box* and the coeditor, with Jaime Cantrell, of *Out of the Closet, into the Archives: Researching Sexual Histories*. Stone's areas of study include lesbian, gay, bisexual, and transgender politics and the incorporation of LGBT individuals into communities and cities, and the law. She lives in Austin, Texas.